African American Food Culture

Food Cultures in America
Ken Albala, General Editor

African American Food Culture
William Frank Mitchell

Asian American Food Culture
Jane E. Dusselier

Latino Food Culture
Zilkia Janer

Jewish American Food Culture
Jonathan Deutsch and Rachel D. Saks

Regional American Food Culture
Lucy M. Long

African American Food Culture

WILLIAM FRANK MITCHELL

Food Cultures in America

Ken Albala, General Editor

GREENWOOD PRESS

Westport, Connecticut • London

Library of Congress Cataloging-in-Publication Data

Mitchell, William Frank.
   African American food culture / William Frank Mitchell ; Ken Albala,
general editor.
         p. cm. — (Food cultures in america)
   Includes bibliographical references and index.
   ISBN 978–0–313–34620–0 (alk. paper)
  1. Food habits—United States.   2. Food preferences—United States.
3. African Americans—Food.   I. Albala, Ken, 1964–   II. Title.
   GT2853.U5M57   2009
   394.1'20973—dc22   2008050411

British Library Cataloguing in Publication Data is available.

Library of Congress Catalog Card Number: 2008050411
ISBN: 978–0–313–34620–0

First published in 2009

Greenwood Press, 88 Post Road West, Westport, CT 06881
An imprint of Greenwood Publishing Group, Inc.
www.greenwood.com

Printed in the United States of America

The paper used in this book complies with the
Permanent Paper Standard issued by the National
Information Standards Organization (Z39.48–1984).

10   9   8   7   6   5   4   3   2   1

The publisher has done its best to make sure the instructions and/or recipes in this book
are correct. However, users should apply judgment and experience when preparing recipes,
especially parents and teachers working with young people. The publisher accepts no
responsibility for the outcome of any recipe included in this volume.

Contents

Series Foreword

If you think of iconic and quintessentially American foods, those with which we are most familiar, there are scarcely any truly native to North America. Our hot dogs are an adaptation of sausages from Frankfurt and Vienna; our hamburgers are another Germanic import reconfigured. Ketchup is an invention of Southeast Asia, although it is based on the tomato, which comes from South America. Pizza is a variant on a Neapolitan dish. Colas are derived from an African nut. Our beloved peanuts are a South American plant brought to Africa and from there to the U.S. South. Our French fries are an Andean tuber, cooked with a European technique. Even our quintessentially American apple pie is made from a fruit native to what is today Kazakhstan.

When I poll my students about their favorite foods at the start of every food class I teach, inevitably included are tacos, bagels, sushi, pasta, fried chicken—most of which can be found easily at fast food outlets a few blocks from campus. In a word, American food culture is, and always has been, profoundly globally oriented. This, of course, has been the direct result of immigration, from the time of earliest settlement by the Spanish, English, French, and Dutch, of slaves brought by force from Africa, and later by Germans, Italians, Eastern Europeans, including Jews, and Asians, up until now with the newest immigrants from Latin America and elsewhere.

Although Americans have willingly adopted the foods of newcomers, we never became a "melting pot" for these various cultures. So-called ethnic cuisines naturally changed on foreign soil, adapting to new ingredients and popular taste, but at heart they remain clear and proud descendants of their respective countries. Their origins are also readily recognized by Americans; we are all perfectly familiar with the repertoire of Mexican, Chinese, and Italian restaurants, and increasingly now Thai, Japanese, and Salvadoran, to name a few. Eating out at such restaurants is a hallmark of mainstream American culture, and despite the spontaneous or contrived fusion of culinary styles, each retains its unique identity.

This series is designed as an introduction to the major food cultures of the United States. Each volume delves deeply into the history and development of a distinct ethnic or regional cuisine. The volumes further explore these cuisines through their major ingredients, who is cooking and how at home, the structure of mealtime and daily rituals surrounding food, and the typical meals and how they are served, which can be dramatically different from popular versions. In addition, chapters cover eating out, holidays and special occasions, as well as the influence of religion and the effect of the diet on health and nutrition. Recipes are interspersed throughout. Each volume offers valuable features including a timeline, glossary, and index, making each a convenient reference work for research.

The importance of this series for our understanding of ourselves is several-fold. Food is central to how we define ourselves, so in a sense this series will not only recount how recipes and foodways serve as distinct reminders of ethnic identity, binding families and communities together through shared experiences, but it also describes who we have all become, as each food culture has become an indispensable part of our collective identity as Americans.

Ken Albala
General Editor

Acknowledgments

In 2006 The Amistad Center for Art & Culture at the Wadsworth Atheneum presented the exhibition *Soulfood: African American Cooking and Creativity.* We hoped the exhibition of visual art, artifacts, and music would help visitors appreciate the creative aspects of African American heritage cooking. In many ways it was the perfect exhibition, and it was the catalyst for this project. The Amistad and Atheneum staff—especially Olivia, Rehema, Monica, Vivian, Ulrich, Zen, Steve, Mark, Cecil, Mary, Jon, Jack, Steve, Allen, Adria, Charlene, Anne, Hugh, Ritz, Efraim, Sharon, and Deirdre—made this project possible logistically and intellectually.

Ken Albala, general editor for the Greenwood Press Food Cultures in America series, and Wendi Schnaufer, senior acquisitions editor, surely showed me more patience and grace during this project than I deserved. Aileen Bastos and Reggie Solomon helped track down photographs and credits. Friends at several libraries shared resources, but I couldn't have finished without access to the Yale library system, New Haven's Public Library, the Connecticut State Library, the New York Public Library, and collections at the University of Michigan and Harvard University.

A wonderfully, diverse and interdisciplinary community of food and history friends offered guidance, conversation, critique, sources, and the sustenance that made the process fun. Jill Cutler, Sharron Conrad, Psyche Williams-Forson, Paul Zolan, Bun Lai, Claudia Highbaugh and Dolores Highbaugh, Teri Rofkar, Serena Epstein, Michael Doolittle, Martien and Neal Halvorson-Taylor, Lauren Berdy, Liza and Al Cariaga-Lo, Bill Curran, Chef Bobo, Susan Pennybacker, Aaron Goldblatt, Josh Viertel, Maryann Ott, Bitsie, Clark,

Mimsie Coleman, Barbara Lamb, Tom Griggs, Ed Bottomley, Hazel and Allen Williams, Becky Abbott, Daisy Rodriguez, Ginny Kozlowski, John Drennan, Stacy Stoller, Rosie Primous, Wendy Battles, Elsie Chapman, and the teams at Birdcraft, Shalom, and cabaret all shared meals, lessons, skills, and enthusiasm.

New Haven, Connecticut, has a rich culinary history based in its multiethnic neighborhoods and these days there is more interest in that history. A devoted crew of historians and activists are organizing the stories from African American, Italian American, Puerto Rican, Anglo Yankee, and other communities to narrate city histories around the state. Their efforts have made New Haven an ideal environment for food studies dialogues: I am grateful to colleagues at the Hartford Studies Project, Stone Soup, Common Ground, Cityseed, Yale's Sustainable Food Project, and the New Haven Food Policy Council. These days our analysis of food is easily contextualized in terms of our health and the planet's. For their good humor in allowing me to introduce an analysis of food and daily life into any conversation, I am indebted to Kate Steinway, Deb Riding, Oliver Barton, Claudia Merson, Claire and Frank Criscuolo, and my research partner Kristin Hass.

Finally, I have to thank the people, particularly the women, who made me curious about food and cooking as a child: Evelyn Audrick, Janie Gray, Janice Smith, Rachel King, Sarah Powers, Lydia Mitchell, and Mary Floyd. My family, John, Judy, and Mike, make meals an education and an adventure. And my mother, Betty, who while fascinating me with stories, recipes, and meal preparation, showed me a kitchen-counter version of interdisciplinary scholarship.

Introduction

EARLY AMERICAN FUSION COOKING

For the Africans forcibly brought to the Americas during the slave trade era, the inventive use of local products and the appearance of familiar and unique ingredients made it possible to shape a distinctive cuisine we now call African American, although authenticity has been subjective and debated from the moment that gourmands and critics claimed the cuisine. African American foodways, an early fusion cuisine and one of the first ever tasted in America, integrate European, African, and American Indian culinary traditions. And like so many other aspects of American culture, African American culinary traditions are in constant motion.

The nation has grown dramatically in the centuries since those first African captives came to America, changing its economy, culture, and food. Foodways may seem insignificant when compared with the momentous obstacles that faced enslaved Africans, but food has played a pivotal role in African American history that encompasses personal nourishment, communal economic mobility, and the agricultural trade that supported the nation. Culinary culture became a defining and unifying construct, almost a symbol, for African Americans, people whose ancestors survived the Middle Passage journey into slavery to build America.

FOOD AND AFRICAN AMERICAN IDENTITY

One of the most controversial books of 2008 was the memoir of a former South Central Los Angeles gang member. The book's press tour began with an interview in the Thursday edition of the *New York Times*. The author welcomed the reporter to her Eugene, Oregon, home to discuss her memoir, a story of gang violence, drug dealing, prison, and death. The author, American Indian and Anglo, reminisced about her adolescence as a foster child in a working-class, African American family and defended the book for its own defense of the family bonds created by choice and by blood. The author, photographed in hooded sweatshirt, jeans, and tennis shoes and seated by her primly dressed young daughter, worried over the public's easy identification of South Central Los Angeles with violence and drugs. She hoped her book would be an eloquent response.

Because it ran in the Thursday House & Home section, the article also described the meal the author had cooking during the visit. "The house smelled of black-eyed peas, which were stewing with pork neck bones—a dish from the repertory of her foster mother, known as 'Big Mom' whose shoebox of recipes she inherited."[1] Later the author prepared a well-practiced, buttermilk cornbread from memory. This article, positive book reviews, and even radio interviews celebrated the book over the weekend. The following Tuesday a *New York Times* front-page story announced *Gang Memoir, Turning Page, Is Pure Fiction*. It should not have been a surprise. The stunt cooking was all wrong. Big Mom's black-eyed peas and pork neckbones were too casual a meal to cook or to serve when being photographed for a national newspaper profile. It may have been expertly prepared, but it tasted thick with insincerity even in the description. The woman had actually lived a privileged life in suburban Los Angeles and had convinced herself that a fake gang memoir with the fish-out-of-water perspective would bring credibility to the stories of friends she had made as a social service volunteer.

If she had lived the history she claimed, then this article, the favorable reviews, and the scheduled book tour would have been an incredible vindication and a celebration worthy of a good cut of meat. She understood the significance of food and its ability to legitimate, but she misread the details of the meal—black-eyed peas do not necessarily go with everything. Because black-eyed peas and cornbread are associated with African Americans, they are ideal props for ethnic performance. Simply to mention black-eyed peas, collard greens, or another signifying food can convey an aura of authenticity for someone hoping to prove their cultural insider credentials. But rules govern how ceremonial food is prepared and when it is presented, and the ability to read, understand, and challenge those rules is a cultural legacy. Authentic food, even when deployed traditionally in cultural or symbolic events, is difficult to define, but a meal can be presented accurately. Similar baked goods are served at breakfast and for dessert, but discerning diners know when a muffin is more appropriate than a slice of cake.

Even more complicated are the food-related rules associated with formal events and rituals, especially those with a religious orientation. Funerals, weddings, and other religious special occasions may have culinary traditions that require strict adherence. The pie that is gratefully accepted by the mourning family of a conservative African American Baptist minister could be inappropriate for the mourning family of a conservative rabbi. By following a recipe, a good cook could make delicious black-eyed peas, but she would need more than a recipe to understand all that the dish conveys.[2] The significance of those traditions is drawn from familiar tastes, the secrets of producing them, and the rules that govern their appearance at holiday meals, on weekends, or even at lunch. Those rules, tastes, and kitchen secrets are as important as a particular food or recipes that may change, evolve, or disappear as a result of history, popular culture, the economy, or medical realities. The recipes alone can yield a delicious meal, but an appreciation of the biographies reveal how and why the food mattered and when or where it changed.

While finishing a dissertation, I taught introductory African American Studies classes at a small liberal arts college with few students of color. The course included a unit on food and cultural identity, and it was a favorite part of the class. The unit culminated in a shared meal that we prepared with recipes from popular African American cooking memoirs. Everyone enjoyed the idea of cooking and sharing the meal they delighted in calling the "soulfood" dinner. For many of the students in that class, the meal we prepared was an exercise that reaffirmed African American biological destiny. We were doing something that black people do. In fact preparing these foods with traditional recipes is something black people used to do. Whether the meals are cooked at home or ordered at a restaurant, African American heritage foods are evolving along with the community these foods represent. Black America is rich with many kinds of diversity. People with different economic, religious, regional, educational, political backgrounds, and even different countries of origin can be described as black Americans.

Some respondents to a recent Pew Research Center survey disputed the idea of a single or unifying black community, citing the growing importance of class differences.[3] A descendant of enslaved Africans and a recent immigrant, both visually black American, can enjoy the culinary and political tradition that accompanies a consciously defined soulfood dinner. The meal, invested with 40 years of political symbolism, is an occasion for those who remember the recipes, stories, and ideologies to pass them along to others. Symbolic or signifying foods remain relevant by reinforcing culture and memory, as they are not transmitted through biology. The food is simply food, its authenticity hard to gauge, but its preparation and the memories elicited by its taste are as authentic as anything can be.

FOOD, IDENTITY, HISTORY, AND BIOLOGY

Medical research continues to shape expectations regarding the sense of taste. Health psychologist Linda Bartoshuk has studied highly sensitive supertasters, the effect of age on taste buds, and sweet tooth genetics. One day there may be a verifiable hypothesis to explain conjectural relationships between cultural identity, particular tastes, and styles of food preparation. Healthier, chemically based alternatives to the sugary, fatty tastes that are so dangerously delicious may be a result. These enduring foods and styles of preparation deliver tastes immediately identified with memories of family. They may not be biologically determined, but they are culturally nurtured as the writers Sallie Tisdale, David Masumoto, and others have suggested in memoirs that explore the boundaries between taste and memory.[4] Beyond the metaphors and memories of living subjects, Hampshire College biological anthropologist Alan Goodman's analysis of ancestral bone material and tooth structure identifies changes in diet and environment.

As an advisor for New York City's African Burial Ground Project, Goodman used dental morphology to locate the region of origin for skeletons of enslaved Africans buried in Lower Manhattan in the 1700s. Certain tastes leave a lasting emotional impression, and it seems that some foods leave a nearly permanent physical impression that can be examined long after the meal and the life have ended.[5] Food fads change, but familiar tastes and acquired cooking instincts are a constant. Mixing certain spices and oils instead of side meat to produce memorably flavored green vegetables, or following a trusted kitchen mentor's baking secret for biscuits will always yield food that seems traditional in sentiment and taste. The survival of this kind of knowledge—the proper taste and the secrets required to produce it—is as important to African American culinary traditions as any favorite dish or recipe.

African American foodways are one of the nation's first and most popular culinary fusions. Many of the best-known recipes unite the cooking traditions and influences of the diverse people who founded America. Many of those dishes have become prototypically American fare, but the style of preparation, taste, and cultural knowledge that surrounds these foods locate them in a broad and encompassing African American cultural tradition, a culture shaped by the diverse groups of African captives forced to work in seventeenth-century America that continues to grow, change, and acculturate new immigrants. People of African descent have been identified and identified themselves in many ways over the course of American history.

Civil rights activists as far back as the abolitionist era described African America as a nation within the nation. Today that nation is the approximately 36.7 million people who claim African descent. African Americans are heavily concentrated in New York, Florida, Georgia, Texas, California, Illinois, North Carolina, Maryland, Louisiana, and Virginia. The median age is younger than other Americans, but African Americans are less likely to live the long lives of their white counterparts. Education, a motivating goal since slavery, remains important and 80 percent of black Americans over 25 are high school graduates; 17 percent have a bachelor's degree. Black America's median household income is less than the median income for whites, and 26 percent of blacks live below the poverty line. Homeownership rates are increasing and some projections suggest that African American buying power may soon surpass $920 billion. Advertisers spend $1.5 billion to reach black consumers. These realities highlight some of the contradictions within African America. As increasing numbers of men and women earn advanced degrees and enter professions—some finding incredible wealth—residents of many poor, urban neighborhoods still struggle to find jobs with a future, promising educations for their children, reasonably affordable housing, and adequate healthcare.

The contradictions are evident in tangible living conditions and in the intangible realm of identity politics. Differing definitions of African American and black affect electoral political decisions, affirmative action policy in educational institutions, and personal identity within families. Black conveys the breadth of ethnic and international diversity embodied by brown-skinned people in the United States. The 2.6 million immigrants who come from Africa, the Caribbean, South America, the United Kingdom, Cape Verde, and other parts of the world are black, although they may not identify as African American or share the same formative experiences as native-born blacks who have several generations of American ancestors.

Visually, they are black Americans, although some may see themselves as ethnically or nationally distinct from African Americans who are the descendants of enslaved Africans. Ethnic identity and heritage can be proprietary investments, but shared foodways open an innovative space for exchange and understanding between new and older communities. Those exchanges can transpire at markets, restaurants, social centers, and eventually at individual homes. The exchange of symbolic food and the accompanying stories will foster cultural connections that are not the result of biology. Ethnically identified foods are part of a matrix of practices that define culture, and those practices are continually evolving and changing. Although these foods are available all over the United States, a person's familiarity with and appreciation for them is an important biographical clue. Soulfood and other cuisines of the black Diaspora continue to help orient, locate, and welcome people into the dynamic cultural community that is African America.

NOTES

1. Mimi Read, "A Refugee from Gangland," *The New York Times*, Thursday, February 28, 2008.

2. For more on food, symbolism, and ethnicity see Linda Keller Brown and Kay Mussell, *Ethnic and Regional Foodways in the United States: The Performance of Group Identity* (Knoxville: University of Tennessee Press, 1985).

3. Andrew Kohut, et al., *Optimism about Black Progress Declines: Blacks See Growing Values Gap Between Poor and Middle Class*, Pew Research Center, 2007.

4. Linda M. Bartoshuk, "Taste: Robust across the Age Span?" *Annals of the New York Academy of Sciences* 561 (1) 1989, 65–75; Jean Anthelme Brillat-Savarin, *The Physiology of Taste*, 1825. Translated Anne Drayton (New York: Penguin Classics, 1994).

5. Alan H. Goodman, "Toward Genetics in an Era of Anthropology," *American Ethnologist* 34 (2) May 2007, 227–229; Alan H. Goodman, "On the Interpretation of Health from Skeletal Remains," *Current Anthropology* 34 (3) June 1993, 281–288.

Chronology

1470s   Portuguese explorers reach the African continent and begin developing trade relationships in the central and western regions.

1500s   Portuguese traders exploit African political strife and buy conquered Africans to sell into slavery. The English, Dutch, and other Europeans soon charter their own human-trafficking ventures. Approximately 12 million men, women, and children are dispersed during the trans-Atlantic slave trade. Foods they are fed during the journey move from Africa to the New World in a transfer called the "Columbian Exchange."

1607   A party of 104 English colonists funded by the Virginia Company arrives at the James River settlement site and name the community in honor of King James.

1609   Jamestown settlers face the "starving time" when they are at war with Native American Indians and unable to grow their own food. Supplies arrive the next year, but many English die of disease and starvation.

1613   Tobacco is proposed as a potential cash crop. Cultivation requires land and people willing to tend it, and originally these people are indentured servants.

1619   English privateers find Jamestown and trade a group of captive Africans from the Angola region, marking the beginnings of an

American system of slavery that will eventually be defined by African physical characteristics.

1620   The *Mayflower* brings radical Protestant Pilgrims to the area they will call the Plymouth colony. They face a grueling winter and many die, but the survivors plant crops and build homes and the next year they are ready for the harvest celebration.

1647   Virginia's Governor Berkeley attempts to grow rice for export, and other planters follow the example, assisted by enslaved black laborers.

1682   Robert LaSalle claims the southern Mississippi River region for France, calling it Louisiana. Its port will become cosmopolitan New Orleans in 1718.

1685   Rice from Madagascar is introduced to South Carolina and becomes a leading crop, Carolina Gold, in the colony by the eighteenth century. Initially English planters, unfamiliar with the grain, fail in their attempts to cultivate rice.

1700   A royal official reports to the English Board of Trade that enslaved black women effectively use their traditional technology, mortar and pestle, to hull rice.

1719   Traders are commissioned to bring Africans familiar with rice crops and the seeds for cultivation to New Orleans.

1732   Cyrus Bustill is born to an enslaved African woman and an English attorney in New Jersey. He is sold to a Quaker, Thomas Prior, who helps establish Bustill as a baker and later frees him. Bustill receives a commendation for feeding American soldiers during the Revolutionary War and starts a school for black children. His Philadelphia home is an Underground Railroad stop for those escaping slavery. Bustill's career as a baker and a Philadelphia activist is an example for Henry Minton, Jeremiah Bowser, Robert Bogle, Peter Augustine, James LeCount, and James Prosser, founders of Philadelphia's black catering dynasties. Paul Robeson, the activist and performer, was a Bustill descendant.

1776   The Declaration of Independence leads the colonies to war with England.

1783   The Treaty of Paris ends the war.

1791   Thomas Downing is born into a free black family in coastal Virginia where he learned to love and cook oysters. His

Manhattan restaurant, Downing's Oyster House, is a favorite of well-heeled New York shellfish lovers.

1800s   "Uncle" Jimmy Matthews creates Brunswick Stew in Brunswick County, Virginia. Slavery is gradually abolished in New England, New York, New Jersey, and Pennsylvania.

1805   Maryland passes a law imposing new restrictions on free blacks who sell corn, wheat, or tobacco.

1829   Philadelphia banker Nicholas Biddle recites his poem an "Ode to Bogle" in honor of the city's renowned black caterer Robert Bogle, the godfather of catering.

1827   Boston activist and manservant Robert Roberts publishes *The House Servant's Directory*.

1841   Black oyster farmers flee Maryland for New York's Staten Island. They settle in the free black village Sandy Ground. Their arrival leads the farming community on Long Island shore into the oyster business. The settlement becomes a stop on the Underground Railroad for those escaping from slavery.

1848   Tunis G. Campbell publishes *Hotel Keepers, Head Waiters and Housekeepers' Guide*.

1860s   Harriet Tubman, who escaped slavery and led many others to freedom, works as a domestic and cook at a hotel in Cape Elizabeth, New Jersey.

1861   The South secedes from the Union and the Civil War begins. William Tilman, an African American cook on a Union ship, is captured with the crew by a confederate ship. Tillman escapes and brings the Union ship back to New York.

1863   President Abraham Lincoln issues the Emancipation Proclamation, freeing enslaved Africans in rebelling states. Black soldiers are given permission to fight for the Union and the end of slavery.

1865   President Lincoln and Congress end slavery with the Thirteenth Amendment. The Civil War ends. President Lincoln is assassinated.

1866   Malinda Russell, a former baker from Tennessee, publishes her cookbook *A Domestic Cookbook: Containing a Careful Selection of Useful Recipes for the Kitchen*.

1868   The United States ensures equal protection for all citizens with the ratification of the Fourteenth Amendment.

1870   Black men gain the vote with the ratification of the Fifteenth Amendment.

1871   African American caterer James Wormley opens a hotel near the White House. His Wormley Hotel becomes a popular destination for the District's political elite. Wormley's Hotel is the site of secret negotiations between the Hayes and Tilden camps during the disputed election of 1876. The agreement, in Rutherford B. Hayes's favor, is called the Wormley Agreement. While working as a steward in London, Wormley makes his name by serving terrapin to fashionable guests.

1881   Abby Fisher, once enslaved in South Carolina, publishes her cookbook *What Mrs. Fisher Knows about Old Southern Cooking* in San Francisco. She and her husband Alexander run a catering business in San Francisco.

1893   Nancy Green, a cook, takes a job playing Aunt Jemima to sell a self-rising pancake mix at the Columbia Exposition in Chicago. She makes pancakes, tells stories of the old South, and sells orders for the mix. In another part of the Exposition, Frederick Douglass, Ida Wells-Barnett, and other activists protest the event's demeaning portrayals of blacks.

1896   George Washington Carver accepts a teaching position at Tuskegee Institute where he becomes an authority on agricultural issues and the many benefits of the peanut and sweet potato.

1901   The Quaker Oats Company begins operation; Quaker Oats grits follow soon after, eclipsing regional products with a national brand.

1910   The National Urban League is organized in New York City as the Committee on Urban Conditions Among Negroes. A year later the Committee merges with two other groups to form the National League on Urban Conditions Among Negroes. The Urban League helped southern migrants adjust to their new homes in the urban North. The migrants had to understand new schools, neighborhoods, jobs, etiquette, and even food.

1917   The United States enters World War I.

1920   Economic and cultural forces converge in The Great Migration, a major population shift for black America that pulls approximately 1 million blacks from the rural South to the urban North.

White theater owners who hire black performers organize as The Theatrical Owners and Bookers Association (TOBA) in Chattanooga, Tennessee. Black entertainers work in poor conditions at segregated theaters in Atlanta, Washington, D.C., New York, Philadelphia, Baltimore, St. Louis, and Chicago. This theater network is later called the "chitlin circuit."

1926   Quaker Oats purchases Aunt Jemima.

1933   Anna Robinson is hired to portray Aunt Jemima at the 1933 Chicago World's Fair.

1934   Claudette Colbert, Louise Beavers, and Fredi Washington star in the original screen adaptation of Fannie Hurst's novel *Imitation of Life*. In the movie a white widow with a syrup business and young daughter hires as her nanny a black woman with a young daughter and secret recipe for pancakes. Together they open a pancake house and eventually sell pancake mix with Louise Beavers's character Delilah as the product's brand image. Their young daughters grow up to resent them.

1936   Generative blues musician Robert Johnson records the song "Come on in My Kitchen" at one of his first recording sessions.

1937   Zora Neale Hurston's novel *Their Eyes Were Watching God* is published. A love story set in a rural, black, southern town and written in a regional dialect, the book presents Janie's search for true love with a man called Teacake against the backdrop of a fascinating and boisterous town of independent African Americans.

1941   Japanese attack Pearl Harbor, and cook third class Dorie Miller takes over a machine gun on the *USS West Virginia* and shoots down several enemy aircraft.

1943   Uncle Ben's Rice appears on store shelves in New Orleans.

1947   National Urban League staffer Edward Boyd moves to Pepsi and hires a small staff to market the soft drink to black consumers. The ads are notable for the profiles of nationally recognized black leaders.

            James and Robert Paschal open a small lunch counter in Atlanta. Their restaurant, Paschal's, is soon locally and nationally known for its fried chicken and interracial dining. Jazz musicians and Martin Luther King Jr.'s civil rights colleagues become regular customers, leading the brothers to support the protests with food and financial contributions.

1949   Future southern cooking preservationist Edna Lewis begins her professional culinary career when she agrees to become the chef at Manhattan's Café Nicholson.

NAACP leader Walter White scandalously marries white South African fashion journalist and cookbook author Poppy Cannon. Poppy Cannon White writes *The Can Opener Cookbook* in 1951 and the *Bride's Cookbook* in 1954.

1954   In *Brown v. Board of Education of Topeka, Kansas*, the U.S. Supreme Court rules that segregated schools are unequal and so unconstitutional.

1955   Cafeteria worker Georgia Gilmore loses her job because of her support of the Montgomery, Alabama, bus boycott initiated by Rosa Parks and organized by Martin Luther King Jr.'s Montgomery Improvement Association. Gilmore's Club from Nowhere sells meals and baked goods to raise money to sustain the boycott.

The Aunt Jemima restaurant opens at Disneyland.

1958   Sue Bailey Thurman compiles and edits the National Council of Negro Women's *The Historical Cookbook of the American Negro: The Classic Yearlong Celebration of Black Heritage from Emancipation Proclamation Breakfast Cake to Wandering Pilgrim's Stew*.

1959   Director Douglas Sirk directs another film adaptation of the book *Imitation of Life*. Lana Turner, Sandra Dee, Troy Donahue, and Juanita Moore star. Sirk replaces the daring pancake and syrup businesswomen featured in the first film with an aspiring actress and the unfortunate woman she allows to be her maid. The daughters resent them.

1960   Four freshmen at Greensboro's North Carolina Agricultural & Technical College protest segregation with a sit-in at the local Woolworth's lunch counter on February 1. By the end of the month, student sit-in protests are occurring all over the South.

1961   Freedom Riders travel by bus through the South to draw attention to segregated facilities. The bus is bombed and passengers are attacked in Alabama.

1962   Author Amiri Baraka renames the standards of African American heritage cooking Soulfood.

1963   Martin Luther King Jr. gives his "I Have a Dream" speech at
            the March on Washington, D.C. President John F. Kennedy is
            assassinated.

1964   President Lyndon B. Johnson signs the Civil Rights Act of
            1964, outlawing discrimination in public facilities and employ-
            ment.

1965   Civil Rights activist and black Muslim leader Malcolm X is as-
            sassinated.

            President Johnson signs the Voting Rights Act, guaranteeing
            access to the ballot box for black Americans even in places
            where fear and intimidation had prevented voting.

1966   Call-and-response chants invoking Black Power are heard at a
            rally in Mississippi.

            Huey Newton founds the Black Panther Party in Oakland,
            California. The party's objective is to protect the residents in
            urban neighborhoods and to bring their progressive agenda to
            America.

            Los Angeles–based cultural nationalist Ron Karenga introduces
            Kwanzaa, a celebration of the first fruits, and an attempt to
            redirect blacks from Christmas celebrations to a holiday with
            an African focus. Celebrants meet for seven nights between
            Christmas and New Year's for philosophical lessons, gifts, and
            festive meals.

1967   President Johnson appoints Thurgood Marshall to a seat on the
            U.S. Supreme Court.

1968   Martin Luther King Jr. is assassinated before a rally in Mem-
            phis, Tennessee. Riots erupt in cities across the nation.

            The Last Poets form at a memorial for Malcolm X. The out-
            spoken poets lay a foundation for rap and in one poem pre-
            dict that some will watch the revolution on TV with chicken
            in their mouths. It is early evidence of an eventual chicken
            backlash.

            Herman Petty opens the first black owner-operated McDon-
            ald's franchise in Chicago.

1970   The Black Panther Party's sponsorship of a free breakfast pro-
            gram for children in urban areas draws media attention.

1974	Comedian Bill Cosby becomes JELL-O Pudding spokesman. With Burger King Corporation support, William McGhee organizes the Burger King Minority Franchise Association.
1975	Wally Amos begins the designer cookie era with Famous Amos Chocolate Chip cookies.
1977	Ben Vereen stars as the enslaved black Chicken George in the television mini-series *Roots*. Chicken George was a descendent of Kunte Kinte and an ancestor of Roots author Alex Haley.
1984	King of Pop Michael Jackson's hair ignites during the filming of a Pepsi Cola commercial.
1986	The California Raisins, anthropomorphized fruit, adopt the sound and style of the Temptations, the Miracles, the Pips, and other African American rhythm-and-blues singing groups for a popular advertising campaign.
1987	Comedian and activist Dick Gregory introduces the SlimSafe Bahamian Diet, a powdered diet drink mix.
	Black Panther leader Bobby Seale, once known for the chant "off the pigs," prepares to release a barbecue cookbook, *Barbeque'n with Bobby*, after selling barbecue in cafes and bars around Philadelphia. The book's popularity will lead him into culinary marketing with his own barbecue sauce and other products.
	Comedian Bill Cosby takes over duties for JELL-O gelatin.
1988	Clarence Grim argues that black Americans' extreme hypertension rates are the legacy of the Middle Passage where captives who retained sodium survived the journey's deprivations. The descendants' gene pool favored a "salt-sensitive gene," leading to high blood pressure. Historians, scientists, and public health officials dispute and eventually discredit the "slavery hypothesis."
1989	Lowell Hawthorne and his family bring Jamaican foods to northeastern black neighborhoods when they open the Golden Krust Caribbean Bakery, a quick service chain serving meat patties and other Jamaican specialties in the Bronx, New York.
1992	Pepsi Co executive Larry Lundy purchases 31 New Orleans Pizza Hut restaurants in the largest African American franchise start up. Warren Thompson buys 31 Washington, D.C., area Bob's Big Boy restaurants.

1993	Six black secret service agents file a discrimination lawsuit against Denny's to protest their humiliation at an Annapolis, Maryland restaurant. It is the third discrimination suit filed against the company that year. Denny's recovers to become a leader in promoting diversity among customers and employees.
1996	Gerry Fernandez, in partnership with General Mills, establishes the Multicultural Foodservice and Hospitality Alliance to promote diversity and inclusion in the foodservice and hospitality industry.
	A consortium of healthcare organizations develops the DASH diet (Dietary Approaches to Stop Hypertension), a meal program with large servings of low-fat dairy, fruits, vegetables, and whole grains to combat hypertension.
1997	Aetna Insurance's annual African American history calendar celebrates Food and Nutrition: From Survival to Choice. Future calendar themes are based on healthy lifestyle issues.
	Soul Food, a movie from first-time director George Tillman Jr., follows the lives of three Chicago sisters as they try to continue the tradition of their mother's Sunday family dinners. Entertainer Gladys Knight's son Shanga Hankerson opens the restaurant Gladys Knight/Ron Winans Chicken and Waffles in downtown Atlanta.
1998	Paul Engler and his Texas Cattlemen lose a defamation suit against Oprah Winfrey for her show on mad cow disease that the cattlemen claim caused a market plunge resulting in an $11 million loss.
	U.S. Surgeon General David Satcher begins the *Control Your Diabetes for Life* campaign to encourage the 2.2 million African Americans with diabetes to continue monitoring blood sugar levels and to educate others who could be at risk.
1999	Starbucks Coffee and basketball legend Earvin Magic Johnson make a deal to open a Starbucks Coffee shop on 125th and Malcolm X Boulevard in New York's Harlem. The partnership calls for seven shops in black neighborhoods in cities with theaters run by Johnson's Johnson Development Corporation.
	Gladys Knight establishes The Elizabeth Knight Fund with The American Diabetes Association to honor her mother who died from complications of type 2 diabetes in 1997.

2002   The popularity of hip-hop artist Busta Rhymes's hit song "Pass the Courvoisier Part Two" noticeably improves the cognac's sales figures.

2005   Hebni Nutrition Consultants release the Soul Food Pyramid, a multicultural interpretation of the USDA food pyramid.

            The District of Columbia makes Emancipation Day, April 16, 1862, the day Abraham Lincoln freed enslaved blacks in Washington, D.C., an official public holiday. Food bloggers wonder what foods should be served for a reinstated holiday.

            Former Illinois Senator Carol Mosley Braun founds the company Good Food Organics and the brand Ambassador organics to produce and market a line of organic teas, spices, and coffees.

2006   Restaurateur and lifestyle guru B. Smith's becomes the brand image for Betty Crocker Cornbread mix. Hip-hop artist and record executive Jay-Z threatens to boycott Cristal champagne when an *Economist* magazine article suggests the champagne company's managing director might want less attention from hip-hop stars.

2007   Ian Smith, African American physician and celebrity journalist, issues the 50 Million Pound Challenge to highlight better nutrition, exercise, and preventive medical care for African Americans. State Farm Insurance is a major sponsor of the 50 Million Pound Challenge national tour.

2008   Neo Soul singer Angie Stone partners with pharmaceutical giant Eli Lilly and Company for the Fearless African Americans Connected and Empowered (F.A.C.E.) Diabetes campaign to help prevent diabetes or better manage the condition in those who are already diagnosed.

            New York City mayor Michael Bloomberg and National Basketball Association star Shaquille O'Neal announce that New York City will be the first to implement nutrition standards for foods served in schools, shelters, youth programs, and other city agencies. O'Neal's efforts to fight childhood obesity include the television show *Shaq's Big Challenge* and the Web site www.shaqsfamilychallenge.com.

1

Historical Overview

African American heritage cooking exemplifies the historical trajectory of blacks in America. Although African American cookery is less celebrated or analyzed than music, dance, visual art, language, or literature, its rules and customs transcend the formal boundaries of history, art, and culture. Emerging under slavery as cultures, people, and resources connected, nascent foodways moved through history to the present, making spiritual, pop cultural, nutritional, financial, and professional contributions to African American life and history. At times it has been a burden. Culinary traditions have been a fertile source for anyone hoping to lampoon African Americans, and some food-related commercial imagery that appeared harmless to marketers has had long-term implications. The African American culinary complex of favorite or traditional foods, folklore, commercial endeavors, and commentary captures the story of blacks in America.

Contact between captive Africans, European Americans, and Native American Indians created the opportunity for blacks to bring their culinary skills and creativity to new materials under trying conditions. They developed a new culinary vocabulary while learning a new language and environment. Successive generations of enslaved blacks refined the ways they cooked and the foods they ate. Those choices, some conscious and others compelled, defined regions and styles of cooking. The most skilled or lucky parlayed culinary prowess or marketing experience into a business opportunity. Foodservice fortunes propelled the sons and daughters of black caterers into their own elite class in the years after the Civil War. They attended prestigious private schools and graduated into the professions. Others struggled to find dignified employment in freedom, for many blacks' experience was limited to the plantation.

Northern factory jobs appealed to hardworking farmers, pulling thousands of blacks to the urban north during the Great Migration in the early years of the twentieth century. Migrants brought their foodways with them, and they found hungry workers with more money and in need of choices. Opening a formal business was daunting, but there were many ways to make and sell meals in black neighborhoods without the prototypical restaurant. After the migrants' journey north with traditional foods, they discovered new culinary experiences in other neighborhoods, at work, and in programs run by social service agencies and community centers. Improvements in the country's food industry and the imperatives of war rations and other food policies forced many Americans to eat differently.

The modern Civil Rights movement reframed African American heritage cooking as food became political in the service of the movement. Women made and sold meals to fund protest activities. Students sat-in at lunch counters to protest segregation. Protesters made spirituals their struggle music as they promised to sit at the welcome table. Political activists served lunch to black children in urban neighborhoods. And a revolutionary poet nationalized the cuisine, calling it soulfood. African American heritage cuisine began its intense and symbolic conversation in kitchens in the Chesapeake region, on the Georgia and South Carolina coast, and in Louisiana in debates over plantation meals for the owners' family and enslaved African workers. *The food can still prompt emotional conversations about identity, health, spirituality, and the significance of these products in the marketplace.*

AFRICANS AND THE JOURNEY TO AMERICA

Although the traditional view of European and African contact is of an interaction structured by exploitation, some scholars argue that Africa and Europe were both active agents in developing an Atlantic world of commerce and the compulsory migration of the trans-Atlantic slave trade. Arab merchants developed historic trade centers along the West African coast long before the Europeans made contact. Trade between Portugal and the Canary Islands in the fourteenth century increased European knowledge of Africa's resources through commercial relationships with conquering African societies. Colonization, religious conversion, growing labor needs, and the market for labor-intensive sugar cane drove European explorers farther south into the African continent. As the currency for payment progressed to include gold and then captive African people, continued European expansion was inevitable. From the fifteenth through the nineteenth centuries, slave merchants took 10 to 12 million African people, many from the areas of Ghana, Ivory

Coast, Senegambia, Benin, Sierra Leone, and Liberia, and sent them on the horrific Middle Passage voyage to the Americas. Many died in transit, but those who survived conceived the African Diaspora's hybridized cultures.

The capture and trade in Africans centered on the western coast of the continent. Because of their proximity to Cape Verde and Portuguese explorers, Africans in particular areas of the continent were already familiar with non-native fruits and vegetables. By the eighteenth century many knew of limes, mangoes, bananas, coconuts, and other tropical fruits that grew along with okra, black-eyed peas, yams, rice, millet, and sorghum. Chile peppers, maize or corn, and peanuts made trans-Atlantic crossings earlier from South and Central America to Africa. Some of these foods had easily identifiable relatives that Africans discovered during or after the Middle Passage. Unlikely as it seems, sometimes foods that were familiar to the captives did accompany them on the journey to the new world. Their captors found that familiar foods made it easier to ensure minimal nourishment for the Africans during the passage. Feeding the captives continued the transfer of seeds now known as the Columbian Exchange. Ships that carried corn, onions, potatoes, and other New England crops to the Caribbean returned from Africa with beans, rice, millet, yams, and other foods that crewmembers fed the captives. These ventures brought several very different worlds into contact.

The emergence of New World Creole or an African American culture was an affirmation of identity and humanity during slavery. Between the journey and their first years in the Americas, captive Africans negotiated the new environment from the most basic details of daily survival to the remote imaginings of an actual future. With so much that had been familiar lost for the African captives, the beginnings of a redefined culinary practice were significant as a language for claiming identity, and eventually in distinguishing skill, trade, work and class opportunities and cultural patterns. In America captive Africans and their generations, free or enslaved, would find routes to autonomy if not actual freedom through the nation's stomach. At markets, on rice plantations, with sugar crops, and in kitchens, blacks in America created a sustaining culture based on and stratified by the nation's culinary needs. Through food service, enslaved blacks found a degree of liberty they ultimately translated into actual freedom. The inspiriting examples are the enslaved black chefs who helped define the young nation's formal cuisine by managing the kitchens of the first Virginia-based presidents, George Washington and Thomas Jefferson.

As president and citizen, Thomas Jefferson was an innovator and a tastemaker, especially at home in Charlottesville, Virginia. He entertained regularly at his home and laboratory, Monticello, and the letters and diaries of many travelers attest to his gracious hospitality. After her 1789 visit to Monticello, novelist and social leader Margaret Bayard Smith described the hearty breakfast she enjoyed at Jefferson's table.

Our breakfast table was as large as our dinner table; instead of a cloth, a folded napkin lay under each plate; We had tea, coffee, excellent muffins, hot wheat and corn bread, cold ham and butter. It was not exactly the Virginia breakfast I expected. Here indeed was the mode of living in general that of a Virginian planter.[1]

She was not the last guest to leave Monticello impressed. Other visitors also commented on the surprising menus that combined elegant French recipes with simpler, farm fare. Several diners made special mention of the ice cream—a rarity for the period—that Jefferson served. Jefferson's table was the ideal theater for presentations of products from his lab. The statesman-farmer imagined the meals to be served at his homes, but he did not cook them. James Hemings, an enslaved black man was responsible for the meals Jefferson enjoyed. James, and later his brother Peter, set a standard that Jefferson took with him to the White House in 1801, but there a French chef did the cooking with the assistance of Edith Fossett and Fanny Hern who had come from the plantation. In appreciation for his service, Jefferson freed James Hemings five years before he won the presidency. Smith also noted that:

The whole of Mr. Jefferson's domestic establishment at the Presidents House exhibited good taste and good judgment. He employed none but the best and most respectable persons in his service. His maitre-d'hôtel had served in some of the first families abroad, and understood his business to perfection. The excellence and superior skill of his French cook was acknowledged by all who frequented his table, for never before had such dinners been given in the President's House, nor such a variety of the finest and most costly wines.[2]

At Monticello Jefferson had 150 enslaved blacks, and many worked along Mulberry Row, the road of workshops, storage, and housing. Jefferson took 19-year-old James Hemings abroad during his term as minister to France. Hemings apprenticed with a French chef and his sister, Sally, trained as a lady's maid. James Hemings ran the kitchen at Jefferson's residence in France and returned to America as the chef at his homes in Philadelphia and at Monticello. James later trained his brother Peter who succeeded him. Jefferson and the Hemings brothers formed a dynasty of enslaved black kitchen staff with French culinary training. Later Edith Fossett and Fanny Hern ran the kitchen at Monticello after Jefferson's retirement. Guests arrived with culinary expectations of a cuisine the lexicographer Daniel Webster once described as half Virginian and half French.

George Washington's chef Hercules accompanied the general from Mount Vernon to Philadelphia—then the nation's capital—to cook for him in 1790. A Washington descendant described him as, "a dark-brown man, little, if any, above the usual size, yet possessed of such great muscular power as to entitle him to be compared with his namesake of fabulous history."[3]

A regular visitor remembered, "Under [Hercules's] iron discipline, woe to his underlings if speck or spot could be discovered on the table...or if the utensils did not shine like polished silver....His underlings flew in all directions to execute his orders, while he, the great master-spirit, seemed to possess the power of ubiquity, and to be everywhere at the same moment."

From 1790 to 1796, Hercules's cooking set a fine dining standard for the nation's first presidential table. Hercules's leftovers may have brought him several hundred dollars a year in takeout service income. Unwilling to return to a Virginia plantation after his years in Philadelphia, Hercules ran away toward freedom a day before citizen Washington left for Mount Vernon. Although Hercules never returned to Mount Vernon, Washington's will legally freed him in 1801. Black chefs continued to set dining standards for American presidents at their personal tables and at the White House into the twentieth century. Fashionable ladies and gentlemen adopted the custom and kept black—enslaved or free—domestic help through the first half of the nineteenth century.

Kitchen staff at Monticello, Mount Vernon, and other large southern plantations defined elegant dining, but they also cooked the meals that visitors believed were characteristic of regional fare. These cooks had permission to experiment with the best ingredients in whatever amounts the household could afford. Washington and Jefferson dined well because of their enslaved black kitchen staff, and in this instance they seem to have shared the wealth. Monticello and Mount Vernon had liberal food ration policies. Enslaved blacks families received whole animals and not simply fat meat or other poor cuts in their rations. This degree of logic in portioning the rations was rare, but adequately reveals the vagaries of daily life for enslaved blacks. Most blacks in eighteenth- and nineteenth-century America balanced the little time and money they had for food with boundless creativity, ingenuity, self-sufficiency, and a pinch of righteous indignation for survival. Cooking or working at a president's residence was refined work when compared with the experiences of other enslaved blacks in Virginia's tobacco farming areas, the rice-growing region of the Carolinas, or New Orleans. Large black communities in each of these regions nurtured an indigenous culture evident in daily practices like cooking style and meal preparation.

THE COLONIAL VIRGINIA PLANTATION

Diaries, letters, biographies, cookbooks, journals, and pantry inventories reveal the kitchen secrets of wealthy families. Clear documentation of the foods enslaved blacks ate is the occasional ledger of dry goods assigned to a family. Oral accounts and biographies add detail to the description of meals. The accepted image of the food given to enslaved blacks—that it was not very good and there was not much of it—is basically accurate, but slavery was regionally specific and influenced by many variables. What foods the enslaved ate is another example of that specificity. Some did eat cornmeal, buttermilk porridge sweetened with molasses, and the infrequent greens and salt meat. But many found ways to hunt, fish, garden, and barter a more varied, tasty, and nearly nutritious diet for their families.

Virginia's enslaved black community began as a response to the labor needed to cultivate tobacco. Native American Indians' familiarity with their Virginia landscape guaranteed that they would not be forced to work on land they knew better than the English. Trial and error proved to the Tidewater and Chesapeake region colonists that tobacco would be their fortune. By the mid-1600s, small farmers and their European indentured servants labored together in family units to bring in a tobacco crop. As the farmers' fortunes grew, their labor requirements increased while their indentured workers received their freedom and bought their own land. Native American Indians could not be compelled to work for the English tobacco farmers, and enslaved blacks from the Caribbean arrived with the knowledge and experience required to grow labor-intensive crops. As wealthy Virginians arranged their social hierarchy, they expanded the previously small pool of enslaved black laborers to meet a growing demand for tobacco.

In the mid-1600s, this small black population, like New England's small black population, accepted the cultural norms of their numerically dominant English enslavers. As this small population grew to include captured Africans, enslaved blacks born in the Caribbean, and enslaved blacks born in Virginia, an increasingly diverse population struggled to build a common culture in the early eighteenth century. Previously residents of the Gold Coast, Senegambia, Sierra Leone, and Benin, the Africans may have had a similar worldview but did not share a religion, language, adulthood ceremonies, notions of family, or household structure. To live together they needed new cultural practices for life in America, and they would integrate aspects of the familiar with what they could use in their current situation. What they found in America shaped the culture they created as much as anything they brought with them.

As African captives grew more familiar with their new lives in America, they understood that both men and women had food procurement duties that could differ from the duties they remembered in Africa. The highly choreographed and gender-specific agricultural roles men and women performed in some African communities became much simpler in America. Men hunted, fished, butchered, grilled, and took other jobs suited to their outdoor skills and mobility. Women cared for gardens, prepared daily meals, and remained closer to the plantation where they might also come across opportunities to supplement a subsistence diet. Virginia's landscape supplied resourceful inhabitants with many opportunities for healthy eating. Enslaved blacks could approach their Native American neighbors for help in negotiating the natural world. These assets made a diet of domestic or wild plants and animals along with corn or another grain, and pork or beef plantation rations a reasonable presumption for enslaved Virginians on a prosperous plantation.

Individual plantation culture and the work requirements of a crop shaped the meal plans. On some plantations a cooking staff fed everyone, but on others individuals fed their own families. Virginia's dependence on tobacco crops imposed the order of the workday for enslaved blacks. The seasonal intensity of the crop cultivation forced enslaved workers to eat easy-to-carry foods that could be quickly prepared such as cornmeal patties heated in coals or roasted potatoes during the busier periods when the tobacco had to be harvested and cured.

Enslaved African cooks brought their traditional preparation techniques to the foods they found in the Americas. Familiarity with millet porridge could be easily transferred to Native American chickahominy grits made from corn. Classic stewed or one-pot meals easily accommodated the tobacco production work schedule, and preparation techniques that included baking, hot fat deep-frying, grilling, or steaming with leaves and ashes suited American food. Africans encountered new plants that became food such as greens—including collards—potatoes, beans, corn, and squash, as well as deer, raccoon, squirrels, oysters, fish, and other animals. Traditional cooking techniques enhanced the flavors of these new foods. The combination of cooking techniques, easy daily recipes, and new favorites created a foundation for more adventurous cultural evolutions as the heterogeneous groups claimed a unifying identity.

Food and leisure were equally important currencies for plantation life, and enslaved workers made time to tend a garden, hunt or trap part of a meal, or sell their produce. As foodways came to symbolize larger cultural relationships, blacks and whites leveraged food as an independent symbol. The act of giving or withholding food could have multiple meanings, as did the way an enslaved black took or prepared food. Beyond the food that plantation owners provided for sustenance, there were also luxury food items that might be given to enslaved workers as rewards or incentives. Tea, coffee, spices, flavorings, specialty fruits, nuts, liquor, sugar, and candy were unavailable to most blacks unless they worked in the kitchen. But they knew these things existed, and enterprising brokers found ways to sample the treats with or without permission.

Mundane foods were easier to come by, and some enslaved blacks took food from the plantation's kitchen garden or a chicken coop for a treat, out of hunger, or to punish the plantation owner. Researchers at Monticello continue their work on the Hemings' era kitchen for evidence of culinary resistance, theft, work stoppage, or little examples of rebellious activism that signal dissatisfaction even in a prized plantation assignment at a model plantation. The enslaved cook's sense of entitlement in the kitchen made some level of retaliation or resistance a seductive option. Standard tales in folklore from the slave era are based on stolen chickens and poisoned plantations. The stories exaggerate reality, but plantation owners' fears of kitchen plots and aggressive rebellion were justified by colonial Virginia's early eighteenth-century history of revolt by enslaved blacks. For black Virginians, food was a critical touchstone in the journey from African captives to enslaved African Americans. Culinary practice united African, European, and Native American influences to produce a new American cuisine. It was a symbol of identity, freedom, celebration, and retaliation. And it was edible.[4]

Eventually, eighteenth-century Virginia planters had enough native-born, enslaved blacks to perpetuate the institution, and the need for recently captured Africans decreased. The African customs embodied by recently enslaved Africans grew more distant. African American traditions maintained by native-born, enslaved blacks became normative. Language, worship, celebration, and food were important ideological manifestations of the sustaining culture that Afro-Virginians created. Although influenced by Anglo-American expectations and structured by an African context that was reinforced by an extended black community, the culture was African American. A large and indigenous African American community enriched familial relationships, worship style, and foodways as one or two isolated black laborers in a seventeenth-century town had grown into an extended network of hundreds of often related black workers on various plantations in an eighteenth-century town.

Recent archaeological research has added to the catalog of data on diet and culinary practices for enslaved blacks in the Tidewater region. Faunal remains discovered at the sites where enslaved blacks once lived confirm that many had access to different and better kinds of food. The excavated remains recovered at one site include wild and domestic mammals, fish, birds, reptiles, seeds, and shellfish marked, cut, or burned in ways that imply meal preparation. Analysis of these bones, shells, feathers, cartilage, and other remnants adds new detail to the earlier accounts of foods the enslaved ate and ways those meals may have shaped an emerging culture.

Archaeologists believe that enslaved blacks understood their status in America through sophisticated interactions with Native American Indians, European American workers, plantation owners, and restrictive laws. As racial norms and racist beliefs emerged, social interactions and cultural patterns were inscribed with meaning and difference. Food, despite its scarcity at times—early waves of Virginia colonists had starved—could be racialized, too. Despite nineteenth-century Virginia's limited range of food options, poorer whites avoided some foods—although they were plentiful and accessible—if enslaved blacks also ate them. In this way both enslaved blacks and poorer whites recognized a collective identity expressed in this case through food-ways: blacks in Virginia's Tidewater region ate possum and fish, but whites, regardless of class, did not.[5]

RICE CULTURE IN SOUTH CAROLINA

Conditions in the Chesapeake-Tidewater areas of the mid South supported a specific culinary culture for enslaved and free blacks. Work requirements in other American regions fostered different culinary patterns for black workers.

Scattered along the coast of South Carolina and Florida are Edisto Island, St. Helena Island, Daufuskie, and others known collectively as the Sea Islands. The region's profitable rice economy produced a distinct cultural and culi-nary tradition. Enslaved blacks in the Carolina Low Country established this rice industry through their tireless cultivation of Carolina Gold rice. In the isolated Low Country, enslaved blacks followed work patterns similar to those used to grow tidal rice in West Africa. A cultural artifact built on the neces-sities of work, Gullah is the hybrid, African and American language and culture of the Sea Islands. Enslaved workers also managed indigo crops and cotton, but rice defined the region and gave the people an identity.

The swampy climate of eighteenth-century South Carolina's Low Country made the plantations fertile but physically uncomfortable. Owners and their families lived in comfortable city homes leaving black workers and overseers to care for the crops. Black workers outnumbered white inhabitants by the mid-1700s. This arrangement permitted a diverse black population, many from the ethnically dense Senegambia region of West Africa, to develop a work language that combined African and English grammatical tendencies. Contemporary Sea Island residents still speak a version of that language, and the cultural traditions thrive in daily exchange and special celebrations.

The exact moment and the circumstances of the rice seed's introduction to South Carolina agriculture remain uncertain. The Carolina Gold seed resem-bles seeds from Madagascar, and researchers believe that it had multiple points of contact on the continent before it proved to be a viable crop for South Carolina. In the 1600s, Virginia farmers believed they had found a kind of rice that would grow on drier land. They had greater success with tobacco. By 1700, South Carolina's Rice Council could promote Carolina's rice industry with news of the year's 300-ton rice shipment to England. Agriculture enthusi-ast Thomas Jefferson promoted Carolina rice during his years in France, where the grain was a popular dessert ingredient. Carolina rice had become one of the new state's leading crops in the years after the American Revolution.

Cultivation of this rice crop allowed enslaved workers an unprecedented level of autonomy for the South. Enslaved Africans in the Low Country lived as families and kept their own schedules. With the seasonal requirements of rice farming, they balanced opportunities for fishing, hunting, gardening, and other chores. Traders brought many of these people to South Carolina because of their rice farming knowledge and their history with O. *glaberrima*, a rice grown along the Niger River in tidal areas of West Africa's Sierra Leone, Guinea, and Gambia. Africans put their skill and adaptive technology to the task of farming rice in America. They pressed their ancestral tools into service to grow the Carolina Gold: preparing the land with hoes, irrigating with an elaborate network of tree trunks and floodgates, hulling the rice grains with giant, carved mortars and pestles, and cleaning or winnowing the rice with platelike, hand-woven baskets, rice fanners, with a Senegambian lineage.[6]

The availability of the rice made it a popular and abundant foodstuff, but the task system of organizing work combined with the area's natural resources made it possible for a set of cooking impulses to mature into a culinary genre. The black majority was the incubator for culinary and cultural traditions with a strong and resilient Senegambian connection. Men participated in food-gathering routines that took them outside the home. Women's primary responsibilities included domestic chores with meal preparation and gardening as priorities. When Works Progress Administration historians of the 1930s took oral histories from African Americans who had lived during slavery, some

Strawberry pickers, Florida, 1911. Courtesy of the Amistad Center for Art and Culture, Simpson Collection, Hartford, CT. AF 1987.1.3828.

shared stories about the foods they remembered. Respondents mentioned their parents tending to family gardens after a day's work in the field.

A typical garden there might be black-eyed peas, sesame seeds, okra, and other plants grown in Africa, as well as beans, sweet potatoes, collards, eggplants, medicinal herbs, and the family's own rice. Women cooked familiar favorites using the methods of their mothers and passed along aspects of history and tradition to American-born children. For a lunch in the fields, a woman might organize a meal similar to the one her mother or grandmother prepared in the rice fields of Sierra Leone. A rice-based, one-pot meal was convenient and relatively easy to make with garden produce. Rice culture eventually defined antebellum black life on the Sea Islands and the foodways that represent Gullah culture.

LOUISIANA, RICE, AND IDENTITY

Louisiana also developed a rice culture during the colonial period, but as a French colony, it granted different freedoms to enslaved black workers. The specifics of the French rule era made southern Louisiana a tolerant recipient of West African cultural practices. Geographically, New Orleans was one of North America's most southern points, but culturally it could have been the most northern point in the Caribbean. New Orleans racial politics, food, religion, public markets, and even the city's architectural lines revealed its Caribbean heritage. Located at the intersection of several competing cultures, New Orleans easily accommodated the West African captives and the varied traditions they carried to America with them.

In 1719, captive Africans, many from Senegambia, arrived at the place in Louisiana that would become New Orleans. They came on ships that French investors sent to West Africa to abduct rice workers. They cleared land, prepared canals, and erected levees and buildings to make the city a reality. As the regional harbor, New Orleans welcomed commercial products including imported foods, cloth, and captured Africans entering the country and charted the Louisiana-grown products that sailed for other ports. Production of regional crops increased quickly, and the number of enslaved Africans in New Orleans grew as well. Eventually, the labor of enslaved Africans made rice, indigo—another plant grown wild in Africa and used for dyes—cotton, lumber, and sugar profitable commodities for Louisiana planters. By 1732, a French colonial census showed that the African population of southern Louisiana outnumbered the white population by a ratio of 2:1.

Captive Africans in southern Louisiana found receptive living conditions—climate, demographics, work expectations—that reinforced cultural continuity, although like their Sea Island peers, the captives had various interethnic conflicts and cultural differences to subsume if they were to realize a unifying culture. A cultural norm as basic as dining customs—whether men and women were separated for meals or ate their meals in family groups—could be a potential New World conflict ultimately resolved by the planter's rules. French colonial laws in Louisiana recognized the idea of a family structure for African captives. The nuclear family unit was a positive incentive in the orientation to New World work expectations. It also supported African culinary and cultural memory.

As in the Sea Islands, blacks in New Orleans created a distinctly African-influenced New World culture with identifiably West African references in music, language, worship, and food. The Creole patois, a hybrid language that follows rules quite similar to the Gullah language, and many of the foods and recipes identified as Creole all share West African cognates, counterparts, or elements. Enslaved blacks maintained aspects of music and worship through public activities in the city, notably Sunday worship in Congo Square, whether or not the French or Spanish colonial governments sanctioned them. In the Square, syncretic spirituality that would ultimately be expressed as Afro-Baptist or Afro-Methodist in the mid South become vodun, the Catholic-inflected West African religious practice.

Experimentation defined the early years of slavery in southern Louisiana and although enslaved Africans had selected liberties, there were severe punishments for running away, collaborating with Native American Indian enemies, and committing violent crimes. Blacks in Louisiana fished, hunted, trapped, and gardened to supplement their rations like their eighteenth-century peers in other parts of the land. Local produce prepared simply was the basis of their diet. As urban residents with privileges to barter and sell goods, enslaved blacks in New Orleans had easier access to such standard luxury items as sugar, salt, and syrups. They used their modest personal freedoms, the legacy of a commercial port city with histories of French and Spanish rule, and the remnants of their native cultures to organize a broadly African, creolized public culture that was especially evident in the cuisine they created, sold, and shared with the world. The trans-Atlantic culinary practice is evident in as simple a detail as the word *gumbo*, the New Orleans seafood stew thickened with okra that is also the word for okra in some West African languages. Gumbos and other stews or rich soups of thick broth, vegetables, leafy greens, and seafood were often accompanied by rice just as West African cooks served the starchy *foufou* or *ugali* with their spicy stews. *Callaloo*, a traditional Caribbean soup made with greens, okra, spices, and chilies, was another example of the culinary impulse to stew certain leafy greens and okra and use the resulting spicy or sometimes gooey broth as a base for distinctive soups. New Orleans market women embodied these trans-Atlantic culinary relationships. Shouting out the praises of their *calas*, the sweet, deep fried rice fritter that was enjoyed as breakfast pastry, these vendors and their pastries were accepted market figures. The fritter was a delicacy of the Diaspora clearly aligned with the foods cooked by the market women's African ancestors who made their own deep fried bean or black-eyed pea fritters they called *akkras*, *aklas*, or *akaras*. *Calas* were once as popular as the signature beignet breakfast pastry is today. Enslaved Africans in New Orleans shared similar raw ingredients and cooking methods with enslaved Africans in the Sea Islands and the Tidewater/Chesapeake region, although the New Orleanians developed a culinary culture that reflects a history of African resistance to attempts at domination by French, Spanish, and American ideologies.[7]

Both Louisiana and South Carolina inherited the European public market custom, and their ports generated retail activity that fed the intersection of culture, identity, and commerce. The presence of free and enslaved blacks influenced market culture. As vendors, the women who prepared and sold delicacies created a public identity—the market woman—while building their own niche market. Blacks participated in all aspects of the markets: supplying, buying, and selling. In 1819, architect Benjamin Latrobe surveyed the busy commercial center of New Orleans on a Sunday morning. He described a black woman selling oranges, black artisans open for business, and a teen with fowl for sale, among others. His complaint that even on the Sabbath

Advertisement for Cream of Wheat cereal, 1915. Courtesy of the Amistad Center for Art and Culture, Simpson Collection, Hartford, CT. AF 1987.1.3869.

the city's economy sped along with black labor suggests the significance of black vendors to the success of the markets. His index reveals the essential role of the market in supplementing a subsistence existence for black New Orleanians and the importance of maintaining the somewhat independent identities afforded enslaved blacks in urban areas. Black commercial activity could serve white business interests, but too much success carried the implied threat of competition. That fear could lead white business leaders to pursue legislation or intimidation to limit black commercial activity. As early as 1737, South Carolina legislators drafted laws aimed at restricting black vendors. Inevitably, black vendors found ways around these efforts, as their participation made the markets shopping destinations for local residents and tourists. Selling these goods was an essential component of the market vendors' resources and a difficult piece to lose. Vendors similar to those who sold spiced coffee, biscuits, peanuts, or pralines in Charleston, Savannah, and New Orleans would find ways to increase their retail opportunities at public facilities after the Civil War. Some, enslaved or free, with rarefied culinary skills ascended to the next step in the culinary marketplace and found positions as professional caterers or cooks.

CULINARY SKILLS AND THE ROAD TO FREEDOM

Free and enslaved blacks found appreciative homes for their culinary and domestic skills in situations that were an improvement on the plantation kitchen but not as grand as the White House. For some, an assignment as a caterer or in a resort hotel kitchen was a step in the larger journey to freedom. Hotels up the Atlantic coast into New England needed experienced workers and hired them whether they were free, enslaved, or escaped. The anonymity of the jobs made them easy places to hide. Catering also seems to have been a fertile training area for activists and aspiring entrepreneurs. Harriet Tubman, the escapee from slavery who led many others to freedom on the Underground Railroad, worked at resorts in Cape May, New Jersey, to earn money for her rescue efforts in the early 1850s. Some workers used these resources to buy their own freedom or the freedom of family members. Black Charlestonian Robert Roberts moved to Boston where, in 1825, he became Massachusetts governor Christopher Gore's butler. Roberts wrote the influential guide *The House Servant's Directory, or A Monitor for Private Families: Comprising Hints on the Arrangement and Performance of Servants' Work* two years later. Roberts' antislavery activism prevented his continued employment in the service field, but his property investments provided a steady income.

During the Civil War era (1861–1865), some fortunate and prepared blacks managed to expand the individual culinary professional niche into viable businesses that could support others. The Philadelphia caterer Thomas J.

Dorsey, who escaped slavery in Maryland, established himself as the city's leading proponent of elegant dining. He amassed a fortune through catering, becoming one of the wealthiest blacks in America. His example encouraged a fraternity of black culinary workers that included Henry Jones and Henry Minton. Robert Bogle and Peter Augustin preceded them and their vision enabled the existence of nineteenth-century Philadelphia's black middle class. In his study *The Philadelphia Negro*, W.E.B. Du Bois called the black caterers "as remarkable a trade guild as ever ruled in a medieval city. The caterers took complete leadership of the bewildered group of Negroes, and led them steadily on to a degree of affluence, culture and respect such as has probably never been surpassed in the history of the Negro in America. This was the guild of the caterers."[8]

Philadelphia Caterer's Chicken Croquettes

2 cups finely chopped or
food processor-ground
cooked chicken
(Can use boneless, skin-
less chicken breasts or try
canned salmon)
3 cloves minced garlic
Plain Panko breadcrumbs
1 tablespoon finely chopped
celery
1 tablespoon chopped parsley
1/2 medium size red onion
finely chopped

2 tablespoons finely
chopped carrots
1/2 cup flour
1 cup warm skim milk
1/2 teaspoon lemon juice
1/4 teaspoon black pepper
1/4 teaspoon sage (only with
poultry)
3 tablespoons butter
1/4 cup olive oil
Safflower oil for frying
Corn meal for baking

Melt butter with olive oil in a sauté pan and add garlic, onions, carrots, and celery and cook for a bit. Slowly add flour and stir until it is mixed into vegetables. Add milk slowly and stir as it thickens and liquid cooks down. Toss in pepper and sage once the mixture looks like a sauce. Salt can be added too if health allows it.

In a bowl mix chicken, parsley, lemon juice, and sauce mixture in intervals, mixing until it is moist enough to make into little patties. Once the chicken mixture has been made into patties, roll them in breadcrumbs until they are well covered. Croquettes can be deep fried or baked on a cookie sheet dusted with corn meal in a 400° F oven for 15–25 minutes.

Tennessean Malinda Russell published her collection of recipes for cooking at home, *A Domestic Cookbook: Containing a Careful Selection of Useful Recipes for the Kitchen*, in 1866. Abby Fisher, another Charleston native born into slavery, published her definitive cookbook, *What Mrs. Fisher Knows About Old Southern Cooking*, in 1881. Mrs. Fisher's comprehensive book includes familiar recipes from southern plantation kitchens, as well as the mainstream recipes that may have been especially popular with her catering clients. Her book skillfully negotiated the emerging revisionist historical interpretations of slavery populated by kind masters, contented slaves, and devoted black women cooks. A marketing campaign for a pancake mix introduced at the 1893 Columbian Exposition codified the once evanescent associations between black women, sentimental depictions of slavery, and the delicious meals produced from their labor. Nancy Green, endearing storyteller, previously enslaved, and a skilled cook, performed Aunt Jemima—a character with dubious origins—and served pancakes at one of the fair's more popular booths. Green helped the Davis Milling Company sell thousands of pancake mix orders and began the immortalization of the Aunt Jemima figure.

Aunt Jemima's pancakes, Rastus's Cream of Wheat, and Uncle Ben's Rice all effectively captured and repackaged commonsense notions of black culinary expertise drawn from slavery. The brand icons brilliantly eclipsed a slave

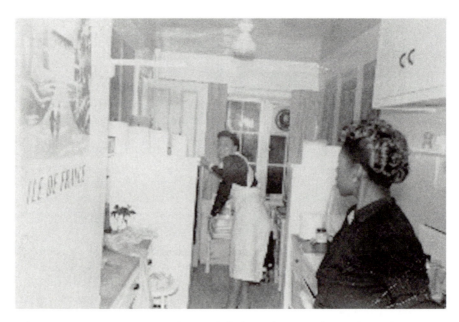

African American women's culinary skills have been in demand. Kitchen scene, 1946. Courtesy of the Amistad Center for Art and Culture, Simpson Collection, Hartford, CT. AF 1987.1.4614.

past, despite the presence of rice, bandanas, and other symbols with direct connections to slavery, and reduced the independence that culinary mastery afforded Hercules or the Hemings brothers through their service to presidents. Popular advertising campaigns for Aunt Jemima and Rastus subsumed knowledge of the culinary and service traditions that created a nineteenth-century black middle class in the North and South. The brand icons did not reflect the intrepid nature the real cooks shared or the ingenuity, ambition, and stamina required to make money cooking and serving meals. This intellectual repositioning of imagined cook for real cook mirrored a physical repositioning of black service professionals, cooks, caterers, and barbers, domestic staff members, who by the end of the nineteenth century were being replaced by new immigrants from Europe.

FOOD AND THE GREAT MIGRATION

In the early twentieth century, millions of African Americans began a slow but steady trek around and out of the South to New York, Philadelphia, Chicago, and other northern cities. People took advantage of the new freedom and moved after the Civil War (1861–1865) and Reconstruction (1865–1877). They moved from the plantation into bigger towns or started independent African American towns. A few moved to cities or headed toward the West Coast. But a generation after slavery in the early years of the twentieth century, most African Americans lived in the South. With the end of Reconstruction, repression returned and many blacks already demoralized by work as sharecroppers, tenant farmers, and domestics faced the terrorism of Jim Crow segregation and crushing discrimination. Several natural disasters left landowners and their tenant farmers in a precarious state. When the World War I (1914–1918) economic boom created factory job vacancies, civil rights and black social service agencies announced that they had workers ready to fill those jobs. By 1920, approximately 1 million black Southerners had moved from the rural South to the urban North.

The Great Migration fostered an urban northern variant of rural southern culture as African American southerners took their music, religion, customs, and cooking across the country and adapted to their new surroundings again. For those who remained to farm the land they owned or contracted to work, life continued to be difficult and most patterns including the culinary remained the same. The most fortunate farming families, like those depicted in Zora Neale Hurston's 1937 novel *Their Eyes Were Watching God*, had the resources to grow more than they could eat and canned or preserved their farm-fresh produce to eat throughout the year. Chef and cookbook author Edna Lewis spent her childhood in Freetown, Virginia, a black farming community started by freed people after slavery ended. Her grandfather was a founder of the town. A resourceful farming family, they only bought sugar and kerosene. She remembered:

whenever there were major tasks on the farm, work that had to be accomplished quickly (and timing is so important in farming) then everyone pitched in, not just the family but neighbors as well. And afterward we would all take part in the celebrations, sharing the rewards that follow hard labor. The year seemed to be broken up by great events such as hog butchering, Christmas, the cutting of ice in winter, springtime with its gathering of the first green vegetables and the stock going away to summer pasture, the dramatic moment of wheat threshing, the excitement of Revival Week, Race Day, and the observance of Emancipation Day.... Whenever I go back to visit my sisters and brothers, we relive old times. And when we share again in gathering wild strawberries, canning, rendering lard, finding walnuts, picking persimmons, making fruitcake, I realize how much the bond that held us had to do with food.[9]

Migrants carried those memories as they moved from rural areas into southern major cities where they created a market for an urban version of their rural or country favorites. In cities large enough to support an economically stratified black neighborhood, someone ran a small restaurant or club with live music, fried fish, barbecue, and other comfort foods that migrated along with the people. These canteens served as godparents of the migration as they supplied multiple opportunities for the aspiring rural worker to know and to covet the city's goods and possibilities. That knowledge meant the move to a larger urban area was inevitable. Once a southerner decided to move north, another network helped facilitate the journey. Train porters, black newspapers, business leaders, and political brokers were all migration advocates ready to help travelers heading north. Train porters formed the center of a service network based in the travel industry, an environment that was segregated and hostile for black travelers. As the industry added food service to some train lines, male porters inherited tasks that had belonged to black women. For certain train routes, enterprising women adapted the market peddler model and sold easily managed food at train stations to fortify hungry travelers. The most influential were the women of Gordonsville, Virginia, who sold fried chicken, coffee, and biscuits to passengers through train windows. The waiter carriers were so prominent that magazines and newspapers profiled them and the town licensed and taxed them. Dining car porters eventually made them obsolete. But their legacy endured in the fried chicken box lunches blacks carried to avoid the humiliation of Jim Crow segregation while traveling.[10]

Black leaders in northern cities recognized the benefits of the larger population base and found new ways to advance migration. Black Chicago's newspaper, the *Chicago Defender*, promoted migration and even gave new urban residents advice on cultural differences they would encounter. Columnists offered their wisdom on how to dress, what to cook, and what was appropriate behavior in public. The National Urban League, The National Association for the Advancement of Colored People, and other new nonprofit advocacy groups helped recent migrants negotiate the cities and in some cases brokered relationships that brought black workers into northern factories. Urban League staff conducted research on living conditions for the new migrants and used the studies in lobbying efforts to improve neighborhoods and job prospects. The combined success of these efforts created or strengthened the African American neighborhoods in New York City, Chicago, Detroit, Pittsburgh, Hartford, Cleveland, Philadelphia, and Boston. And in these new predominantly black neighborhoods filled with poor, working, and professional people, shops that prepared and sold the food that signaled memories of home slowly appeared.

FOOD, IDENTITY, AND POLITICS

Analysis of African American cultural products transformed by the migration experience—music, worship style, language, visual art, literature, athletics, theater—often ignores food. The cultural revolution of the late 1960s corrected the omission, reminding cultural historians of the overlapping boundaries between African American foodways and southern food.

In the early 1960s, the cultural nationalist poet Amiri Baraka (1934–) coined a phrase to describe the urban version of African-American heritage cooking. Soulfood was the perfect symbol for a black cultural revolution. Fried chicken, barbecued ribs, pork chops, fried fish, collard greens, candied sweet potatoes, potato salad, cornbread, and other familiar foods were symbols that connected African Americans across a spectrum of diversity. The magic of the foods and the memories they evoke were mystical enough to make strict definitions difficult. Soulfood was another cultural product, possibly the most symbolic, with a strong historical lineage. People knew it had southern roots and that workers, if not enslaved blacks, had eaten something like it. That sense of history was an affirmation of community as its members prepared for the changes to come. Changes they expected from the legislation, court orders, and presidential decrees that would make America a nation based on equality. In the tumultuous era of the modern Civil Rights movement, African American foodways strengthened identity as people wondered about these changes. As soulfood, this sample of favorite foods from the African American southern kitchen gained a new identity charged with the political obligations of the Black Power era. The new name brought African American foodways back into the twentieth-century celebration and analysis of African American culture.

NOTES

1. Margaret Bayard Smith, *The First Forty Years of Washington Society: Portrayed by the Family Letter of Mrs. Samuel Harrison Smith from the Collection of her Grandson, J. Henley Smith* (New York: Scribner and Sons, 1906), 69.

2. Bayard Smith, 391.

3. George Washington Parke Custis, *Recollections and Private Memoirs of Washington, by his Adopted Son G. W. Parke Custis . . .* (Washington, D.C.: W. H. Moore, 1859).

4. Monticello researcher Lucia Stanton has described the combination of cooking and resistance as hostile cooking. For research on African American Monticello see Lucia Stanton and Dianne Swann-Wright, *Getting Word: The Monticello African-American Oral History Project* (Charlottesville: Thomas Jefferson Foundation, 2006); Woody Holton, *Forced Founders: Indians, Debtors, Slaves, and the Making of the American Revolution in Virginia* (Chapel Hill: University of North Carolina Press, 1999); Rhys Isaac, *The Transformation of Virginia, 1740–1790* (New York: W. W. Norton & Company, 1982); Philip J. Schwarz, *Twice Condemned: Slaves and the Criminal Laws of Virginia, 1705–1865* (Baton Rouge: Louisiana State University Press, 1988); Larry McKee, "Food Supply and Plantation Social Order: An Archaeological Perspective," in *I, Too, Am America: Archaeological Studies of African American Life*, ed. Theresa A. Singleton (Charlottesville: University of Virginia Press, 1999).

5. Maria Franklin, "The Archaeological and Symbolic Dimensions of Soul Food: Race, Culture and Afro-Virginian Identity," in *Race and the Archaeology of Identity*, ed. Charles Orser (Salt Lake City: University of Utah Press, 2001).

6. Daniel C. Littlefield, *Rice and Slaves: Ethnicity and the Slave Trade in Colonial South Carolina* (Urbana: The University of Illinois Press, 1991); Titus, Mary, "Groaning Tables and Spit in the Kettles: Food and Race in the Nineteenth-Century South," *Southern Quarterly* 20 (1992): 13–21; Karen Hess, *The Carolina Rice Kitchen: The African Connection* (Columbia: University of South Carolina Press, 1992); Judith Carney, *Black Rice: The African Origins of Rice Cultivation in the Americas* (Cambridge: Harvard University Press, 2001).

7. Thomas N. Ingersoll, *Mammon and Manon in Early New Orleans: The First Slave Society in the Deep South, 1718–1819* (Knoxville: The University of Tennessee Press, 1999); Anne L. Bower, *African American Foodways: Explorations of History and Culture* (Urbana: University of Illinois Press, 2007); Gwendolyn Midlo Hall, *Africans in Colonial Louisiana: The Development of Afro-Creole Culture in the Eighteenth Century* (Baton Rouge: Louisiana State University Press, 1992).

8. W.E.B. Du Bois, *The Philadelphia Negro: A Social Study* (Philadelphia: University of Pennsylvania Press, 1899), 32. Also see Lawrence Otis Graham, *Our Kind of People: Inside America's Black Upper Class* (New York: HarperCollins, 1999).

9. Edna Lewis, *The Taste of Country Cooking* (New York: Alfred A. Knopf, 1976), xxi.

10. Eric Arnesen, *Brotherhood of Color: Black Railroad Workers and the Struggle for Equality* (Cambridge, MA: Harvard University Press, 2001); Joe Trotter, *The Great Migration in Historical Perspective: New Dimensions of Race, Class, and Gender* (Bloomington: Indiana University Press, 1991); Psyche Williams-Forson, *Building*

Houses out of Chicken Legs: Black Women, Food, and Power (Chapel Hill: University of North Carolina Press, 2006); Tony L. Whitehead, "Sociocultural Dynamics and Food Habits in a Southern Community," in *Food in the Social Order: Studies of Food and Festivities in Three American Communities*, ed. Mary Douglas (New York: Russell Sage Foundation, 1984).

BIBLIOGRAPHY

Arnesen, Eric. *Brotherhood of Color: Black Railroad Workers and the Struggle for Equality*. Cambridge: Harvard University Press, 2001.

Carney, Judith. *Black Rice: The African Origins of Rice Cultivation in the Americas,* Cambridge: Harvard University Press, 2001.

Custis, George Washington Parke. *Recollections and Private Memoirs of Washington, by his Adopted Son G. W. Parke Custis*...Washington, D.C.: W. H. Moore, 1859.

Du Bois, W.E.B. *The Philadelphia Negro: A Social Study*. Philadelphia: University of Pennsylvania Press, 1899.

Franklin, Maria. "The Archaeological and Symbolic Dimensions of Soul Food: Race, Culture and Afro-Virginian Identity." In *Race and the Archaeology of Identity*, ed. Charles Orser. Salt Lake City: University of Utah Press, 2001.

Gordon-Reed, Annette. *The Hemingses of Monticello: An American Family*. New York: W. W. Norton & Company, 2008.

Graham, Lawrence Otis. *Our Kind of People: Inside America's Black Upper Class*. New York: HarperCollins, 1999.

Hall, Gwendolyn Midlo. *Africans in Colonial Louisiana: The Development of Afro-Creole Culture in the Eighteenth Century*. Baton Rouge: Louisiana State University Press, 1992.

Hess, Karen. *The Carolina Rice Kitchen: The African Connection*. Columbia: University of South Carolina Press, 1992.

Holton, Woody. *Forced Founders: Indians, Debtors, Slaves, and the Making of the American Revolution in Virginia*. Chapel Hill: University of North Carolina Press, 1999.

Ingersoll, Thomas N., *Mammon and Manon in Early New Orleans: The First Slave Society in the Deep South, 1718–1819*. Knoxville: The University of Tennessee Press, 1999.

Isaac, Rhys. *The Transformation of Virginia, 1740–1790*. New York: W. W. Norton & Company, 1982.

Kulikoff, Allan. *Tobacco and Slaves: The Development of Southern Cultures in the Chesapeake, 1680–1800*. Chapel Hill: University of North Carolina Press, 1986.

Lewis, Edna. *The Taste of Country Cooking*. New York: Alfred A. Knopf, 1976.

Littlefield, Daniel C. *Rice and Slaves: Ethnicity and the Slave Trade in Colonial South Carolina*. Urbana: The University of Illinois Press 1991.

Opie, Frederick Douglass. *Hog and Hominy: Soul Food from Africa to America*. New York: Columbia University Press, 2008.

Schwarz, Philip J. *Twice Condemned: Slaves and the Criminal Laws of Virginia, 1705–1865*. Baton Rouge: Louisiana State University Press, 1988.

Smith, Margaret Bayard. *The First Forty Years of Washington Society: Portrayed by the Family Letter of Mrs. Samuel Harrison Smith from the Collection of her Grandson, J. Henley Smith*. New York: Scribner and Sons, 1906.

Stanton, Lucia, and Dianne Swann-Wright. *Getting Word: The Monticello African-American Oral History Project*. Charlottesville: Thomas Jefferson Foundation, 2006.

Titus, Mary. "Groaning tables and Spit in the Kettles: Food and Race in the Nineteenth-Century South." *Southern Quarterly* 20, nos. 2–3 (1992): 13–21.

Trotter, Joe. *The Great Migration in Historical Perspective: New Dimensions of Race, Class, and Gender*. Bloomington: Indiana University Press, 1991.

Williams-Forson, Psyche. *Building Houses out of Chicken Legs: Black Women, Food, and Power*. Chapel Hill: University of North Carolina Press, 2006.

2

Major Foods and Ingredients

African American consumers evaluate food purchases by the same criteria as other Americans: quality, value, taste, and history. People want foods they know how to prepare, they know will be delicious, and they know they can afford. Food that is fresh, familiar, and affordable is a priority. Because so much of the nation's food is processed to be cheap, easy, and recognizably flavored, the preparation of many traditional foods and ingredients is either reserved for special events or its preparation is a special event because of the time required. Many of these meals are labor intensive even when the ingredients are not expensive. The rigorous preparation makes it possible to make a delicious meal from inexpensive ingredients. The meal has value because it is one of the few affordable luxuries. Most people do not cook these kinds of meals without timesaving shortcuts, but the opportunity to cook this way—whether it is weekly, monthly, or yearly—recalls a period in African American history when the freedom to make decisions about meal preparation and the time to prepare meals were symbols of new freedom. In the late nineteenth and early twentieth centuries, many recently freed people finally had control of their bodies, the little they earned for their hard work, their family relationships, and whatever they could grow or forage to eat. Access to ingredients that had been unimaginable helped the best cooks to complete and then proudly share favorite recipes. The integration of food, friends, and farm chores—corn shucking, molasses making, butchering, or the harvesting of a common crop—helped transform the experience of communal work into a celebration of new freedoms.

Today, the effort required to bake biscuits from a recipe or to marinate and fry a whole chicken can be too much. Paying the premium for someone else's baking and frying is an appealing alternative, but that choice turns home cooking into a rare event. Many African American families, wherever they now live, have an association with the agrarian South through parents, grandparents, or other relatives. Generations have spent summers or family vacations visiting with relatives who cooked traditional favorites to celebrate their family visits. The association of black family unity and the rural South endures, but there are threats to this idyllic tradition. The African American rural South is disappearing. The signs of a reverse migration of blacks back to the South have not improved the conditions for African American farmers. The 1 million African American farmers who owned land in the early years of the twentieth century were not self-replicating. There are fewer than 20,000 African American farmers on the land currently, and farming, small-scale urban gardening, or large rural farms seem ideologically exotic. In Detroit and other shrinking cities, some residents are gardening on neighboring lots that were once vacant homes. The Nation of Islam manages the 20-acre Muhammad Farms in southwest Georgia to fulfill Elijah Muhammad's vision of a sustainable agricultural system for black Americans. The loss of African American-owned farmland and the growth of mass-market food and

Community gardeners in Brooklyn, New York, at the Bedford-Stuyvesant Garden Coalition garden. AP Photo/Suzanne Plunkett.

consumer-packaged goods are transforming African American foodways as profoundly as economics, education, and popular culture. The South as an idealized place where African Americans reconnect with family and tradition through heritage foods is becoming a fiction.

The major foods and ingredients described here are historically and ideologically central to African American heritage cooking, but they compete with many other foods that are faster and simpler to prepare. Their relevance in the twenty-first century will depend on the kinds of creative adaptations that kept these favorites on the table during the twentieth century.

MEAT

Meat is the center of the American diet and that is true for African Americans. It is a symbolic and economic indicator of financial stability. Meat and poultry feature prominently in folklore and contemporary comedy as symbols of family unity, prosperity, and spiritual integrity. In his 1945 autobiography *Black Boy*, Richard Wright presents the archetypal hungry preacher at Sunday dinner. At the special Sunday dinner, Richard had to finish his soup before he could have any fried chicken. The preacher had already eaten several pieces when Richard worried aloud, "That preacher's going to eat all the chicken." When comedian Chris Rock seems to joke about the hardworking head of household's need to feel appreciated—give daddy the big piece of chicken—he is recognizing the power of food, chicken really, to confer authority, identity, and honor.

African American cooks are credited with an ability to do more with less, a skill perfected out of necessity, but America's economic transformation during the twentieth century meant that many people had to be creative and thrifty with their food. A dining table analysis of the African American journey from the economic margins toward the financial mainstream would have meat at the center even when it was unaffordable in stores and hunting or trapping was unrealistic. Vegetarianism is increasingly an option for political and health reasons, but many people still expect to see meat on the table at a meal. Americans eat less red meat today than they did 30 years ago, but that meat still weighs in at approximately 200 pounds—red meat, poultry, and fish—per person.

PORK

Pork has fallen from its once sacred place and has become controversial for religious and cultural reasons. The Nation of Islam embraces a dietary law that requires followers to abstain from eating pork. For health-conscious African Americans, rejecting pork is often seen as a necessary step on the road to better living. Black Muslims belong to a faith tradition founded by the charismatic religious leader Wallace Fard who appeared in Detroit in 1930. Three years later he had 8,000 members who supported his Islamic teachings and worshiped at the Detroit mosque. After Fard's disappearance in 1934, his student, the late Elijah Muhammad, succeeded him, and the religious tenets that Fard, Muhammad, and current leader Louis Farrakhan espouse integrate self-determination, economic empowerment, and aspects of traditional Islam. One practice adopted from traditional Islam is the rejection of pork. The Nation of Islam's penetration of black, urban neighborhoods in the late twentieth century could be gauged by the fervent debates about pork and its significance in black culture. More recently Louis Farrakhan has encouraged Nation of Islam followers to practice the strict vegetarianism that was truly Elijah Muhammad's goal. African American converts to orthodox Islam also abstain from pork because it is *haram* or unlawful. People interested in Rastafarianism, Seventh Day Adventists, and some who are committed to healthier eating shun pork, too. Although many criticize pork in political terms—as an unclean oppressor—or worry about its health hazards—a silent killer, others continue to enjoy bacon, ham, sausage, chops, or a pork roast. Ham, salt pork, and other cured meats are essential ingredients for many traditional dishes, but adherence to tradition is now balanced by the growing appreciation of high blood pressure, pancreatic cancer, and other health hazards.[1]

Pork's long-term health implications may be costly, but it is relatively affordable and easy to find. Just as French charcuterie preserves the entire pig carcass by smoking, curing, and salting, every part of the pig is used in the African American culinary tradition. During slavery the most fortunate or resourceful blacks kept their own pigs, were given a pig for rations, or took one. Survival required making the best use of the animal. Smoked, cured, or pickled meat used sparingly could feed a family for seasons. A small piece of cured pork, sometimes called side meat, salt meat, or salt pork, is still used to flavor many vegetables, soups, and stews.

The least valuable parts of the animal are processed for sausage, a food that Africans discovered once they arrived in the New World. Of the various types of sausage, fresh—made with spiced, raw meat that requires cooking—and cooked or partially cooked—to be eaten cold or cooked—are the most popular. British-style sausage flavored with pepper, sage, and other spices is a breakfast favorite. American baloney is a version of Italian cooked salami that is named after the city of Bologna. It is made with spicy, ground pig parts, but the taste barely resembles Bologna's *mortadella* sausage. The hot dog is the final sausage product; it is a standard in most American and African American diets. Baloney or sliced bacon can be substituted for slab bacon or salt pork in a recipe. And baloney, fried or cold, is truly a comfort food. Hot dogs play a crucial role in extending a meal or as a recipe replacement for more expensive cuts of meat. Fried baloney, sausage, bacon, and occasionally a slice of ham are breakfast foods that appear at morning meals, as well as in the afternoon and evening.

Naming and preparing the pig's fatty meat is a science. Fatty meat from the pig's side and back is salted, smoked, and cut into slices for bacon. Unsliced it is slab bacon, which is similar to the salt-cured, but unsmoked fatty layer cut from the pig's stomach and side called salt pork. Salt pork was a preferred seasoning in the preparation of collards and other greens. Fatback is the animal's back fat that is rendered for lard or smoked, salted, or even deep-fried in small pieces for cracklins. And ham hocks are the lower part of the pig's hind legs that have meat, fat, and bone. They are usually cured, smoked, and used to add a rich, smoky flavor to black-eyed peas and other slow-cooking vegetables, soups, and stews. Ham is the cured, smoked, and sometimes dried thigh of the pig's hind leg. Europeans brought their ham recipes to the American South where different trees, new neighbors, and new culinary influences all converged in the recipe for country ham. The ham is dry cured with salt, sugar, and other spices and then smoked for several months before it is ready to be cooked and eaten. The standard is Virginia's Smithfield ham, which is dry salted with salt and pepper, smoked with hickory, oak, or apple wood, and then aged for as long as a year. The Smithfield ham, or one of its imitators, is the ham for holiday and special-occasion meals.

The legacy of smokehouse cooking lives on in the backyard barbecue. South American barbecue customs penetrated the North American continent in the eighteenth century and immediately felt American. No meat is better suited to the barbecue grill than pork spareribs. Spareribs are the fatty meat and bone cut from the lowest section of the pig's rib and breastbone. Marinated or cured, grilled or smoked on the barbecue and detailed in sauce, ribs and the barbecue experience—Georgian, Tennessean, and North Carolinian schools barbecue with pork—are the quintessence of American smokehouse work from previous centuries. Barbecue differs from grilling because it is the slow cooking of meat over low heat that results in a smoky, infused taste. Cooks debate whether the meat should be cooked over a direct or indirect heat, in a pit or modern grill, and with wood or coals. Tennessee barbecue, or really Memphis, is either pork ribs or shoulder meat shredded after hours of barbecue braising. Pork ribs may be served wet, with sauce, or dry flavored only by the seasoning rub. Eastern North Carolina barbecue is a chopped or pulled pork shoulder—at a true barbecue pit the pitmaster cooks the entire hog— that is richly flavored with a vinegar-based sauce and smoked over hickory or another heavily scented wood. Traditional East Texas-style barbecue is made with pork and served with or without sauce, although most Texas barbecue is made with beef and served without sauce. Kansas City, Missouri, barbecue is a version of the now definitive pork sparerib—often served with a rich, smoky, slightly sweet, tomato barbecue sauce—that is a cookout standard across the country. Kansas City was an early and important stop on barbecue's great migration north and west to Chicago, Detroit, Los Angeles, and Washington, D.C. The intersection of several barbecue traditions is evident in Kansas City and reflects its status as a barbecue crossroads.

Pork chops are also cut from the pig's rib but come to the table smothered or simmered with gravy or breaded and fried. Hog maws, chitterlings, and pigs feet are the most notorious cuts of pork. These pieces may have inspired the phrase "high on the hog" because enslaved blacks hoped one day to get more if not the whole pig in their rations. Chitterlings or chit'lins are the pig's small intestines and require fastidious cleaning before they are slow-cooked until tender enough to be eaten. The cleaning is intensive and the cooking releases a memorably pungent smell. Hog maw is the pig's stomach and it must be thoroughly cleaned before cooking. Pig's feet are bony, potentially still hairy, and obviously need to be thoroughly cleaned as well. They can be purchased fresh, smoked, or pickled to season another dish. Chitterlings, pig's feet, and pork neck bones can be stewed for hours with bay leaves, onions, pepper, parsley, or other seasonings, and served with rice. Hot sauce and vinegar are the only acceptable condiments.

BEEF, LAMB, GAME

Historically, pork, poultry, and game have been the meats sought by African American cooks; and they are the meats of recipes, jokes, and stories. Beef's European popularity was not reflected in the United States until the nineteenth century, although beef is now the alternative to pork for abstemious African Americans. Beef baloney, hot dogs, and short ribs are regularly substituted for the fatty, pork versions. Round steak, chuck, shin bone, and some cheaper cuts of beef are stewed, ground for meatloaf, or coated, fried, and served with a gravy. Beef neck bones and oxtails can be simmered for hours with vegetables until the broth becomes gravy. The dish is served, like pork neck bones, with potatoes, rice, or grits. Although a regular meat for North African Muslim cultures, lamb was even more of a rarity for nineteenth-century African Americans than beef. The relative prosperity some families achieved in the early twentieth century made lamb and mutton options for those who lived close to farms or good urban markets. For those who will not eat pork, lamb chops are an easy substitute.

POULTRY

Chicken has a long history of worldwide culinary applications, and although southern fried is one of the most recognized, the bird is not native to

America. Nineteenth-century breeders developed the Rhode Island Red, the Plymouth Rock, and other "American" versions of the animal Darwin called *Gallus gallus*. Until modern chicken farmers found ways to produce birds for mass consumption, chicken dinner was a special treat for the wealthy or farmers. Factory farming of chickens by Perdue, Tyson, and others has made chicken a convenient and inexpensive ingredient for daily meals. Baked, grilled, stuffed, stewed with dumplings, broiled or processed into nuggets, meat pies, or cutlets, chicken is ubiquitous, and like pork or game the history of agriculture and slavery guarantees an economic and folkloric relationship between blacks and chicken. Pork's religious complications and perceived health risks have been the good fortune of chicken farms. Food press coverage of commercial chicken farm outrages, bird flu, and other difficulties in the poultry industry has not spoiled chicken's appeal.

The different parts of a slaughtered chicken, like the pig, were not wasted in the past, so innards, feet, and all were sautéed, stewed, or baked into a meal. But the objective of cooking with chicken has always been a fried chicken dinner. With the various styles of chicken available, baked, roasted, or grilled chicken is easier to prepare. Fried chicken is iconic and it is the correct way to enjoy chicken, and the range of fried chicken recipes reflects regional, ethnic, and historical differences. Prepackaged turkey drumsticks, wings, or other parts, especially smoked, are increasingly popular substitutes for pork in flavoring collard greens, black-eyed peas, and other long-simmering dishes. Turkey and chicken cold cuts, hot dogs, and sausage have become trusted alternatives.

FISH

Fish is a traditional favorite because of its value, convenience, and taste, especially when battered and fried. In season it is not difficult to find fish outside of grocery stores, and fried fish is a delicious and cross-cultural cooking experience. Plenty of women fry fish, but men who are not primary cooks at home will catch, clean, and fry their fish. Members of northeast Ohio's North Coast Black Bass Anglers Association, Detroit's Motor City Bass Anglers, and other black sport fishing clubs hope to inspire those who fish for recreation. There are now fishing programs with a youth diversion emphasis in some major cities as well, but a larger number of African American men in urban centers continue to fish for recreation at the most convenient points, which can be as unlikely a spot as the industrially situated Detroit River. It might also be a secluded fishing spot near western Michigan's summer retreats settled by blacks in the mid twentieth century.

The taste for fish is evolving. A greater appreciation of pollutants in American waterways, concerns about fried food, and the local grocery store's inexpensive farm-raised salmon have altered fish preferences. Grilled salmon is simpler and healthier than a fried alternative. It is frequently ordered in restaurants and prepared at home. As consumers have become more informed about threats to salmon, tuna, and sea bass, the fish most associated with African American culinary history has surfaced in the mainstream. Catfish can be found in freshwater or coastal environments all over the world. Atlantic catfish are legendary, although consumers are likely to buy farmed catfish at the grocery store. The distinctive barbels or feelers around the mouth of the fish resemble cat whiskers; its bones, and its rough, scaly skin can make it difficult to clean and cook. They are cut and sold as fillets to be easily dipped in egg, rolled in cornmeal, and fried. The fish has a delicately mild flavor and is low in fat. Whiting and porgy, both cheap and hearty enough to be fried, are popular alternatives to catfish.

Among the anchovies, sardines, smoked oysters, crab, and other canned fish products, pink salmon and tuna stand alone for their place in the pantries of African American cooks. Croquettes, a nineteenth-century black caterers' specialty, with pink salmon replacing chicken, moved from the public dining room to the family dining room as an easy, economical, and elegant dish suitable for family or guests. Crab, shrimp, and other shellfish were nutritious and convenient meal basics for blacks in towns along the Atlantic coast. During slavery and after, blacks living near Charleston, Savannah, New Orleans, and other coastal cities with public market cultures acquired, sold, and cooked with the seafood that was convenient. That legacy is the inspiration for inventive modifications of familiar favorites. Recipes for the unmistakable shrimp dishes and simmered, mixed seafood stews served in South Carolina, Louisiana, Georgia, and Alabama have been updated for simpler meals that can be made anywhere. Shrimp and grits, fried shrimp, boiled shrimp, gumbo, jambalaya, and Frogmore stew have been adopted far beyond their southeastern home, but the convenience of frozen or canned shrimp makes shrimp salads, cocktails, and platters popular choices, too.

African American residents of the Chesapeake region have a historical affiliation with the seafood business where black participation in the crab and oyster industry dates back as far as slavery. This aspect of aquaculture, like sailing, whaling, and other nautical professions, allowed blacks, enslaved and free, a degree of opportunity, a sense of freedom, and sometimes equality unavailable in most other areas of American life. Enslaved blacks from the coastal areas of antebellum Maryland gained their freedom and headed north where some helped to make oysters fashionable in nineteenth-century New York. Freeborn black oysterman Thomas Downing moved from Virginia's Chincoteague Island to New York where he established one of the city's most popular oyster cellars or rustic restaurants. Downing's restaurant was popular with the political and financial elite who enjoyed his fried and raw oysters.

Free blacks with oyster and farming skills left Snow Hill on Maryland's eastern shore in the mid-1800s hoping to find an area where they could live free from racial restrictions and violence. They found that place on New York's Staten Island in the historic oyster farming area that by the early nineteenth century had a small community of previously enslaved blacks. Through farming and oystering, black residents prospered and made their community, Sandy Ground, a financially and politically thriving center of African American life. The Chesapeake Bay's enslaved black families continued in the oyster and crab industry after the Civil War, and some families opened their own seafood businesses in the early twentieth century. Black waterman tonged for oysters in their boats and women picked crabs in packinghouses, but their children chose lives outside the seafood industry. Today that tradition continues in the adapted recipes for crab cakes and soft shell crabs and the preparations for festive crab boil parties where resourceful cooks flavor the boiling water with their own special spice blend rather than the usual Old Bay Seasoning mix.

GRAINS, STARCHES, AND BREADS

Grains and starchy dishes complement the main course in cooking of the black Diaspora. Millet, sorghum, yams, rice, cassava, corn, and plantain are essential grains and starches in the West African diet. Life in North America made it possible to expand the diet and to substitute North American native foods for those found in Africa. Rice was a familiar foodstuff for some West African captives, especially those from the Ivory Coast and Senegambia regions that had rice-farming traditions. These farmers cultivated a rice species that is native to Africa, *Oryza glaberrima*, and grows well in a tidal environment. Portuguese traders recorded their observations of the technology Africans used in the rice cultivation process during their voyages to fifteenth-century Africa. Rice was one of the provisions served to kidnapped Africans on the Middle Passage journey to the Americas. Sailors gave the captives beans, yams, plantains, peanuts, palm oil, occasionally a little meat, and sometimes corn, but the familiar favorites yams and rice must have been the only comforting reassurance on the journey. Captive Africans from Sierra Leone and neighboring areas arrived in America with their rice farming skills and an appetite for rice. After adjusting to the environmental conditions of the American South, enslaved black rice farmers made the grain a plentiful crop and a culinary standby for blacks in the rice-growing Southeast.

Rice dishes made with Carolina Gold, rice originally from Madagascar, remain definitive symbols of African-derived, southeastern cooking. The peas and rice combination is the most straightforward rice dish to emerge from the African Diaspora, and popular versions appear in black cooking around the world: peas and rice in the Caribbean, black beans and rice in Cuba, or black-eyed peas and rice in America. Red beans and rice is a New Orleans rice-and-beans combination made with kidney beans and a spicy sauce. New Orleans's dirty rice is served in tangy, meat sauce and red rice takes its color from paprika, tomatoes, and red pepper flakes. South Carolinians called these one-pot dishes of rice cooked in a meat-flavored broth, *pilau* or *purloo*. Louisiana's Jambalaya, rice cooked with shrimp, chicken, sausage, and tomatoes; *étouffée* made with seafood, vegetables, and a dark gravy or roux; and gumbo stew of okra, tomato, seafood, chicken, and sausage over rice belong to the *purloo* family.

Corn, corn meal, and hominy grits—dried, ground corn kernels—are native foods embraced and reinterpreted by Europeans and Africans on their arrival in the New World. It is a fine coating for frying chicken or fish, but most often cornmeal is the raw ingredient in cornbread, corn muffins, stuffing, and other savory baked goods. There is a cornbread market and brands are willing to fight for it. General Mills's marketing research suggests that African American consumers purchase 36 percent of the cornbread mix sold in American grocery stores. By targeting its Betty Crocker brand corn bread mix to black consumers, General Mills increased its sales by 23.3 percent, encroaching on Chelsea Mills's popular Jiffy corn muffin mix. For many cooks it is either the cakelike Jiffy mix or cornbread from scratch. In focus groups with black employees, General Mills's executives discovered the many ways their colleagues "doctored" packaged cornbread mixes with fresh corn, buttermilk, peppers, herbs, nuts, and more. General Mills's executives succeeded in attracting black consumers with coupons, celebrity endorsements, and repackaging during the peak cornbread period around Thanksgiving.[2]

Grits, yellow or white, are standard fare at a full breakfast along with eggs, bacon, sausage, ham, and biscuits. They can be served with milk and sugar as a hot breakfast cereal. Grits are made from corn hominy—kernels that have been soaked in an alkaline solution to absorb the liquid, dried, and then ground—in a process pre-Columbian cooks called nixtamalization. Early Aztec and Mayan cooks used ashes for lime when soaking and cooking the corn to soften the kernels, make them easier to grind, increase their nutritional value, and enhance the flavor. Nixtamalized corn is the basis for tamales, corn tortillas, and other favorites from the Southwest and Latin America. The nixtamalization process is thousands of years old, but researchers continue to analyze it for potential improvements in food preparation today. Once the grits are completely processed, they can be simmered in liquid to produce a soft, lightly flavored porridge. Enriched with butter, cheese, herbs, or meat, grits can be eaten after breakfast, too. Leftover grits are an invitation for creativity and can return to the table fried, baked, souffléed, frittered, broiled, and in many other imaginative forms. Instant grits, a finer grind, simplify a full breakfast, which is still where most people encounter grits. The longer-cooking grits are the necessary base for complex recipes.

Biscuits have nearly as many variations as cornbread, and like cornbread the biscuit is versatile enough to be eaten early in the morning, late at night, and at any other time of the day. Buttermilk biscuits are descendants of eighteenth-century Virginia sour milk bread. This biscuit, or its twin made with regular milk, is the base for sausage and creamed gravy, bacon, or ham sandwiches, and strawberry shortcake.

Sweet potatoes grow prolifically in the warmer parts of the country. George Washington Carver, the African American food scientist and inventor, extolled the health benefits and various uses for sweet potatoes. Carver's advocacy made the enjoyment of sweet potatoes a civic duty and they are an affordable, nutritious staple for African Americans. Boiled, baked, roasted, and candied sweet potatoes are fine, but they are best when whipped into custard for pie. Because they are a good source of vitamins A and C, nutrition advocates promote sweet potatoes as one of the healthier foods in African American heritage cooking. White potatoes, fried, mashed, or boiled and diced for salad, are always acceptable. Along with grits and rice they lend texture and balance to the many strong flavors in African American heritage cooking.

VEGETABLES

Enslaved Africans who kept subsistence gardens grew an impressive variety of vegetables. Many of those vegetables appear in family meals today. Okra, which comes from a shrub that is native to Africa, is resilient, grows well in North America, and is rich in vitamins A and C. The firm, green, tapered, pods are filled with seeds and a viscous juice. Okra has a mildly acrid taste that is reminiscent of Brussels sprouts or asparagus, but that flavor mellows with cooking. It tolerates batter and high heat frying, but it also simmers nicely into stews, thickening and adding texture to gumbo. Okra can be pickled, served with rice, and mixed with other vegetables, although its natural companions are corn and tomatoes.

Garden-fresh tomatoes are the foundation for soups, sauces, and even rice dishes. These nightshades are eaten, red and ripe, with bread and mayonnaise or vinegar as a sandwich or green, battered, and fried. They add flavor to soups and are baked or stewed with breadcrumbs and bacon. They are also pickled and preserved in chowchows, jellies, and relishes. Butter beans, lima beans, and green beans have a long history with African American cooks and along with other green vegetables—collard, mustard, turnip, and even dandelion greens—were vanquished by hours of cooking in a salt pork broth known as pot liquor. These leafy greens, especially the nutrient-loaded collards, are found in African-derived cooking around the world. Whether thinly sliced and sautéed in hot oil or chopped and dropped into a meat stew, the greens are savored with hot and vinegary condiments.

The black-eyed pea, also native to Africa, is an influential legume. More than kidney beans, navy beans, or lima beans, black-eyed peas—and the related field peas—are fundamentally representative of African American cooking and the food of the African Diaspora. As fritters, stews, salads, and *purloos*, black-eyed peas have followed black people all over the New World. Fresh-grown peas at markets are rare, although committed gardeners grow them in backyard gardens. For many southerners, black and white, a taste of black-eyed peas on New Year's Day is the only way to welcome the New Year and to invite good fortune.

DAIRY

Lactose intolerance, difficulty with milk digestion, affects the health of African Americans. Misperceptions about lactose intolerance are changing the patterns of dairy consumption. Milk, buttermilk, cream, and butter were indispensable in kitchens for cooking and at the table for eating. Evolving food preferences in twentieth-century America, however, have made buttermilk, once a primary milk product for many blacks, an idiosyncratic, guilty pleasure and the savvy cook's baking secret. Buttermilk is the low-fat chunky liquid produced while cream turns to butter. Adding acidic bacteria to skim milk turns it into buttermilk. The thick milk is a baking reactant found in recipes for biscuits, cakes, and cookies, but the modern manufactured version does not have the same dramatic taste as the actual butter-chunked milk. Fears of maldigestion have not dislodged cheddar and American cheese as favorite flavors for snack foods or as ingredients in macaroni and cheese, cheeseburgers, and similar classic dishes. Ice cream and pudding are classic favorites that tempt even those with digestion issues.

FRUITS AND SWEETS

Baked goods and sweet desserts are central to African American foodways. Sweet potato pie is a prototypical pastry from the African American culinary tradition, and it exemplifies aspects of the tradition by its incredible sweetness, the smooth custard, and the creative use of a sweet potato. Other aspects of the culture are daring or exotic, but the favorite dessert offerings are conservative and familiar. Sweet potato pie is the most radical dessert. Fruit and fruit flavorings are equally important for a memorable dessert. Peach, cherry, apple, lemon, and banana are ingredients in definitive pies, cakes, and cobblers.

Pineapple, coconut, grape, orange, and strawberry are popular enough that artificial versions flavor candies and sodas.

MAJOR TASTES

Foods of the African Diaspora are memorable because of the complex flavors. A well-seasoned dish will usually mix sweet, salty, spicy hot, or vinegary tangy flavors. Barbecue sauce and lemon meringue pie are good examples of a continuum that incorporates salty, sweet, hot, and tangy. To produce those flavor combinations, peppers are necessary; they can be fresh peppers—Jalapeno, Cayenne, Habanero, or Serrano—or a peppery hot sauce. A little cider or white vinegar delivers the desired sharp, acrid taste. Together they bring a fermented pucker to green vegetables, fried foods, and even potato chips before manufacturers sprinkled vinegar and salt flavorings on them. Sassafras and its derivative, file powder, as well as basil, allspice, mace, cinnamon, thyme, parsley, nutmeg, garlic, and sage are all indispensable for properly spiced food. White sugar is the most frequently used sweetener and it is present in all kinds of dishes. Some cooks add a teaspoonful of sugar to the pot when cooking collard greens. Brown sugar is necessary for baking and candied sweet potatoes. Molasses, a residue created during sugar cane processing, is an occasional sweetener along with cane syrup, but commercially packaged maple syrup is the popular choice. These flavors and ingredients are at their best in the relishes, pickles, jellies, and chow chows that some home cooks still prepare annually.

Texture and density enhance the sweet, hot, and salty flavors that characterize the foods that emerged from the African Diaspora. Hearty soups or stews are thickened with okra, dairy-rich sauces, and occasionally pulverized nuts and pastes. Sesame seeds—known as benne or bene in Africa's Senegambia region—add texture to biscuits, candy, and meat or fish as a crusty coating. Peanuts are one of the nuts most closely associated with African Americans and cooking. Peanuts traveled from Peruvian South America to Africa with Portuguese explorers. West Africans called them groundnuts, and the nuts came to the Northern Hemisphere as a result of the slave trade. Peanuts grow easily in sandy soil and the Virginia peanut is one of the most popular varieties. Tuskegee Institute food scientist George Washington Carver's peanut experiments revealed the plant's versatility, although peanuts are still primarily enjoyed boiled, roasted, shelled, in candies, occasionally as part of a meal, and usually as peanut butter.

COOKING OIL

Oil was a foundation of West African cooking, and in America blacks found that pig fat was versatile and plentiful. Pig's fat, or lard, is a necessary foundation of many favorite dishes and its faint, nutty, sweet infusion has proven hard to replace. Lard is the product of rendering, or slowly melting, the pig fat from its skin, organ tissue, and carcass pieces. It was a standard cooking oil but also an essential ingredient for baking flaky biscuits and piecrusts, but this ingredient is often replaced in recipes with vegetable oils, vegetable shortenings, or margarine. Because lard carries health risks that are easier to avoid with other, lower cholesterol options, some have replaced lard with vegetable oil and unsaturated shortening. Shortening can mean butter, lard, or another oil or fat, although it is usually a solid vegetable fat like Crisco—which is cheaply manufactured, easily stored, and amenable to high heat cooking—that produces perfect pie crusts, biscuits, and cookies. Many cooks swear by lard for baking and frying, and it has never been unpopular in some parts of the country. Lard's waning popularity does not mean the end of pork fat for cooking. Many home cooks frugally conserved bacon grease and the oil cooked off from other fatty pork returns to the pan as frying oil. Corn oil, peanut oil, canola oil, safflower oil, and olive oil are also substituted, although nothing shares lard's delicate flavor.

NOTES

1. Elijah Muhammad, "The Truth about Pork (the Pig)." *Muhammad Speaks* October–November, no. 5 (1961).
2. Steven Gray, "Betty Crocker Adds B. Smith to Package for Cornbread Mix, and Sales Take Off," *The Wall Street Journal*, Tuesday, November 14, 2006, B1; Lois A. H. Mosley, *Sandy Ground Memories* (Staten Island: Staten Island Historical Society, 2003); Alan Davidson, *The Penguin Companion to Food* (New York: Penguin, 2002).

BIBLIOGRAPHY

Edge, John T. *Fried Chicken: An American Story*. New York: G. P. Putnam's Sons, 2004.

Egerton, John, ed. *Cornbread Nation 1: The Best of Southern Food Writing*. Chapel Hill: University of North Carolina Press, 2002.

Hakim, Nasir. *Exposing the New Dangers of Pork*. Chicago: Secretarius Publications, 2002.

Harris, Jessica. *The Welcome Table: African-American Heritage Cooking*. New York: Simon & Schuster, 1995.

Muhammad, Elijah. "The Truth about Pork (the Pig)." *Muhammad Speaks* October–November, no. 5 (1961).

Warnes, Andrew. *Savage Barbecue: Race, Culture, and the Invention of America's First Food*. Athens: The University of Georgia Press, 2008.

Wright, Richard. *Richard Wright: Later Works: Black Boy [American Hunger] The Outsider*. ed. Arnold Rampersad. New York: Library of America, 1991.

3

Cooking

Cooking in African American homes today reflects the pervasive influence of America's commercial food culture. Advances in the food industry, targeted advertising, greater disposable income, and broader cultural contacts combine for a contemporary set of expectations about food and its preparation. Differences in how, when, and who prepares meals can be influenced by class, region, and ethnicity. African Americans, like other American consumers, consider convenience, schedule, and value when deciding on meal details. There are constants: women bear a greater burden for meal planning and cooking, men often learn something about cooking from mothers and fathers and can prepare basic dishes, and children have more opportunities to understand cooking and nutrition and they can organize simple snacks or meals.

Many labor-intensive traditional foods are now reserved for special occasions. The canned and prepackaged alternatives are acceptable substitutes for daily meals. Managers in grocery chains and the packaged food industry recognized an opportunity with the prepared foods section. Better prepared foods make it possible for men or women to serve varied and delicious meals quickly and easily every night. With busier schedules and easier meal organization, traditional expectations regarding meal preparation and identity are shifting, too. In a busy two-parent household, the father is now more likely to be responsible for organizing a regular dinner, for the grocery shopping, or another meal-related chore. Prepared food options make dinner decisions easier for shoppers who live in, or have access to, well-run, full-service grocery stores. In too many economically disadvantaged, urban neighborhoods, a modest grocery store, an expensive convenience store, and fast food are the only choices. Some have only convenience stores. Making the trip to a well-stocked market with fresh produce, quality meats, and regularly rotated packaged goods becomes a luxury. Even with limited choices, these shoppers find ways to make meal preparation more convenient.

The narrative for African American culinary professionals does not follow the same theme of progress and transformation. Continued black ownership of quick service restaurant franchise and neighborhood restaurants means blacks will be involved in the industry. For young people a job at one of these restaurants is a solid introduction to restaurant or service industry careers, but only a small number of blacks reach the other side of the food service industry. Few African American students attend prestigious culinary schools and even fewer become leaders in the kitchens of high-profile restaurants. Those numbers affect cooking and dining for African Americans nationally, from the kinds of restaurants located in black neighborhoods to the choice and range of foods that become trends.

SUPERMARKETS AND GROCERY SHOPPING

The American food distribution industry is diverse, adept, and expansive. California and New York, the most densely populated states, share the greatest number of this nation's 66,000 grocery stores, a category that does not include 38,000 specialty markets for meat, cheese, fish, and bakery items. Many shoppers wander through an overwhelming selection of packaged foods offered by an industry that reacts quickly to signs of interest in such trends as organics, exotic scents or flavors, and healthier lifestyles. The grocery store category now includes Target, Kmart, and similar category-bending department, discount, pharmacy, grocery stores, the high-end super stores, supermarkets, and discount clubs. For the right price, American consumers can usually find whatever fruit, fish, spice, or condiment they need whether it is in season or regionally grown.

A grocer's ethnic foods section, stocked with Uncle Wiley's, Glory Foods, and other smaller packagers, clearly illustrates the market's ability to incorporate ethnicity or African American culinary trends. Uncle Wiley and Glory Foods have grown from their initial focus on traditional, southern-style canned vegetables to include healthy seasonings for salads, frozen entrees, bagged and washed fresh collard greens, and heat-and-serve side dishes.[1]

African American consumers value these developments in the market for the freedom they provide, as well as the cultural validation. But after selecting for region and income, they are as likely as other Americans to shop in a grocery superstore with a prepared-foods section, produce islands, in-store coffee bars, and even hand-held scanners to allow the customer to scan and bag items while shopping. And researchers are beginning to notice and record these shopping habits. A. C. Nielsen consumer insights report that African American shoppers purchase more table syrup, sugar, dried vegetables or beans, grains, flour, noncarbonated juice, sweeteners, spices, yeast, deli/packaged meats, frozen unprepared meats, and seafood than other American shoppers.

Market researchers predict that spending by black consumers will push black buying power from 700 billion to the trillion-dollar mark in the next decade. Although only 20 percent of black consumers are identified as affluent, the demographic is responsible for almost 50 percent of black America's purchasing strength. This privileged category is a special target for advertisers, and it is courted in ads that appear in the historical black media and through sponsorship of art exhibitions, Martin Luther King' s birthday, and Black History Month events, and African American Arts and Leisure television programming on PBS, BET, and TV One. This development is good news for the 20 percent of black households with the ability to spend as desired, but the remaining 80 percent may face some obstacles beyond the individual pocketbook and can be underserved by the few poorly stocked, small neighborhood grocers.[2]

African Americans who live beyond high-income zip codes face barriers in the selection of quality food, and those obstacles influence meal choices that can eventually have dramatic health consequences. Transportation, neighborhood demographics, and store merchandise shaped by an inexact customer profile all exacerbate the problem, but food policy advocates blame the urban grocery gap for the food insecurity experienced in many predominantly black, urban neighborhoods. Although most American-born blacks have agricultural production somewhere in the family history, many, especially urban residents, have no direct control over their food sources. How the food is cultivated, where it is grown, the type of transportation that brings food to market, and other factors affect food security and influence food sovereignty, that is, people's right to control food choices and sources rather than having them defined by major corporations. The Philadelphia Food Trust's Supermarket Campaign, the University of Connecticut's Food Marketing Policy Center, and the U.S. House of Representatives Select Committee on Hunger have acknowledged the urban grocery gap phenomenon. Urban areas, especially lower income neighborhoods, are underserved by an inadequate number of full-service grocery stores. In these food deserts shoppers improvise with small independent stores whose managers are unable to stock the wide range of fresh, healthy foods for the same low prices as the large, suburban, full-service grocery stores. If a grocery chain does have a store in a predominantly black neighborhood, there are inevitable questions about the quality of the meat and produce for sale there.[3]

Community development corporations, food policy advocates, and their sponsors in city government assemble incentive programs to attract large grocers to inner-city neighborhoods. Generous packages that offer parking lots and tax abatements are tied to larger planning decisions. Those negotiations are driven by a city's long-term strategy and the neighborhoods identified as promising. As a minor constituency in those dialogues, underserved shoppers need to find solutions that work in the interim. A multidisciplinary consortium of departments led by Carnegie Mellon's Urban Laboratory in the School of Architecture proposed several unique solutions to food scarcity in Pittsburgh's historic African American neighborhood, the Hill District. Students researched and designed a co-op style grocery store for the neighborhood, helped with Geographic Information System mapping to confirm the area's limited grocery store choices, and conducted public health research to study these issues' impact. Although they have thoroughly documented the problem and identified solutions, the Urban Laboratory's Centre Food needs funding and other kinds of municipal support before it can be built.

City farmers' markets are a promising intervention for urban residents, and the number of markets has increased 18 percent since 2004. Freshly harvested, organic produce is expensive even with the Farmers Market Nutrition Program coupons that subsidize fruit and vegetable purchases for eligible families. Other alternatives include neighborhood green grocers, natural foods stores, and some specialty shops. When weather permits, farm stand vans or mobile green grocers appear at swap meet-open air markets, street festivals, and at busy corners in larger urban areas. Their produce may be from another vendor, a local garden, or truly farm fresh depending on the season. These items are cheaper than comparable purchases at any store. In some neighborhoods a small grocery store chain moves into the void while city government pursues major chains and shoppers improvise their own solutions.[4]

Even small chain stores can struggle for survival in underserved neighborhoods, but demographic impact of immigration on a neighborhood profile can improve the prospects. Markets that successfully cater to new immigrant populations increase shopping opportunities for all residents. Until management at larger supermarkets recognizes the potential profits located in historically, underserved areas, customers there will rely on the operators of small stores. Those storeowners will stock the basics and may accommodate a regular customer's financial hurdles. Their customers will pay a heavy service charge to have these amenities conveniently brought into the neighborhood. The ease or difficulty associated with grocery shopping will affect who is responsible for food shopping and who cooks it.

Chicago's downtown farmer's market at Federal Plaza. AP Photo/Darryl Bush.

PERSONAL COOKING

Gender-based expectations regarding women and cooking prevail in African American culture. Women are assumed to be more proficient shoppers and more able cooks, but more men, across the economic spectrum, are responsible for household chores including cooking. In homes with two working adults, especially younger couples, the man is likely to shop for and prepare a meal, although the woman is primarily responsible for organizing the family nutrition agenda for the week, month, and year.

Cultural customs are passed from one generation of women to the next and meal preparation follows that pattern. Black women's social networks and the supporting media encourage the association between women and cooking. Gender-specific family lore and the enticing recipes found in popular women's magazines are transformative ingredients in making a meal that is fast, tasty, nutritious, economical, and different. A growing body of cookbooks focus on African American culinary traditions, and a few are compilations of magazine recipes. The most interesting negotiate traditional cooking styles and contemporary themes to make foods that are healthier, internationally flavored, vegan, or influenced by another food trend. These resources support the continued identification of women with cooking and cultural tradition.

Whether this reflects the reality in every home or even most, African American women are expected to maintain and organize family culture from holidays to weekly shopping and daily cooking.[5]

Men do not have the same onerous sense of responsibility for meal preparation, although many take a task that could be occasional shopping, cooking, or cleanup after the meal. Very few are continuously responsible for all of this even if they had food-related chores—part of a meal prep or cleanup—as teens. For those men who have benefited from strong relationships over multiple generations, few of the shared traditions are related to daily meal preparation. Practical kitchen lessons are likely to have been imparted by a mother or female relative, although boys do see their fathers prepare breakfast, make lunches, and organize a dinner if needed. They are sure to be familiar with whatever meal the father claims as a specialty.

If women do the bulk of the private cooking in the home, men are the public cooks. The physicality of outdoor cooking, particularly grilling, is associated with male cooks and the celebrated barbecue cooks are usually male. The performance of fishing, hunting, and outdoor grilling have rules and standards that are passed along between generations. Cooking a meal is not the ultimate goal in these activities, but well-prepared, good food is important. The pace of daily life and the proximity to hunting and fishing locations make it impossible for every boy to have these lessons. Shopping or cooking with a parent is a more frequent exercise for boys and girls, but boys who have this chance inevitably put the experience to use in later life. Some of the best public cooking is happening at popular men's cook-off or bake-off fundraising events. Participants come from black male fraternal organizations, church groups, government, and local business to show wives, girlfriends, relatives, friends, and each other that men can be great cooks. *Real Men Cook* and similar events showcase men's cooking skills and allow women to revel in a slight role reversal while men boast about their hidden talents. These fundraisers are the most current variant of familiar pancake breakfasts, fish fry dinners, and other purchase-a-meal fundraisers run by men's groups.[6]

The collective male kitchen at a pancake breakfast evokes memories for some crewmembers of military cooking. The military is one of a few major societal institutions that support men's culinary impulses. During the years of military segregation, many black servicemen were relegated to kitchen assignments, although some found opportunities to prove their mettle as soldiers. Dorie Miller, the black cook who shot down several enemy aircraft during the 1941 Japanese bombing of Pearl Harbor, returned to the kitchen after his heroics. A generation of African American military men shared formative cooking experiences. The modern military is a model of diversity and equity, although some societal institutions, most with involuntary admission, still practice coercive cooking. Men who enter with or acquire cooking skills during their incarceration leave with an advantage that some have exchanged to benefit their finances and public profile. In special event, special circumstances, and public cooking, men shine as periodic cooks, but tradition and culture reinforce the expectation that women will assume responsibility for daily meal organization.

Most children's cooking instruction will come through female relatives at home, but concern about childhood obesity, physical exercise, and healthier eating has translated into adolescent cooking lessons delivered to their venues. On television, at scouting events, in after school and camp programs young people discover ways to prepare healthy snacks and light meals as they are drilled on better nutrition tips. A few grassroots programs with ambitious staff attempt culturally sensitive healthier cooking with students. Most are focused on helping young people consider healthier choices and making them realize that every decision, from what is bought at the store to how it is prepared, has implications for their health. The identification of food and health through after-school and camp activities complement the identity and culture lessons that come from cooking and eating at home.

PROFESSIONAL COOKING

In the spring of 1947, a small group of activists, friends of the civil rights leader Bayard Rustin's from the Congress of Racial Equality (CORE), boarded a bus headed south from Washington, D.C., to begin the "Journeys of Reconciliation" to protest segregated facilities. Harassed, beaten, and arrested at several stops, the protesters received a 30-day jail sentence in North Carolina that ended the protest. The same year Jefferson Evans graduated from the Culinary Institute of America. He was the school's first black graduate, and although protesters flooded the South on buses protesting segregation 15 years later, the number of African Americans attending professional culinary schools has not increased radically. Contemporary graduates of prestigious culinary schools choose from the corporate or restaurant worlds. Opportunities in the corporate world—hotels, resorts, restaurant chains, corporation cafeterias—come with all the amenities of secure jobs; the choice of restaurant chef comes with less security but is made more enticing by the star chef dream.

For African Americans the decision to pursue a career as a restaurant chef can be difficult. The best culinary programs are expensive investments, the restaurant world exists on transition, and blacks with apprentice or on-the-job training can become managers of profitable restaurants. Motivated students and their parents imagine a similar investment in a legal or medical education is a better choice and one not biased by the African American history of service. Despite those obstacles, black students choose to enroll in

Chefs Michael Dillard and Michael Branham serve a meal for a New York City community organization. AP Photo/Mary Altaffer.

regional and nationally known culinary programs for the four-year bachelor of professional studies or the two-year associate in occupational studies degree, although the number of black students at the most prestigious schools still hovers between 5 and 10 percent. National Labor Bureau data from 1992 show that blacks held 13 percent of supervisory positions in food service. The National Restaurant Association statistics show that the number increased to 14 percent by 2005, although African Americans owned only 4 percent of dining establishments. This larger community has created a stronger support network for African American culinary professionals. In 1993, a group of black Culinary Institute of America graduates formed the Black Culinarian Alliance (now known as the BCA), an organization for culinary professionals of color. In addition to promoting members and building a network, the BCA honors culinary professionals with the Jefferson Evans award at an annual fundraising celebration. The organization sponsors programming for young people on nutrition and culinary careers. BCA efforts were a catalyst in the creation of mentoring programs and school initiatives to draw more high school students into culinary careers or higher education with a culinary focus. These activities focused attention on professionals who are managing the neighborhood restaurants but also creating opportunities throughout the industry in restaurant groups, hotels, clubs, and as industry consultants. A related organization, the Multicultural Foodservice and Hospitality Alliance (MFHA), emerged in 1996. The MFHA is a nonprofit focused on research and advocacy that promotes diversity to build a more inclusive foodservice and hospitality industry. Their recruitment efforts, scholarship programs, and institution-based advocacy are improving the employment realities in restaurant, foodservice, and hospitality work.

Family restaurants serving customary fare to regular diners are the foundation of African American professional cooking. The culinary tradition that poet activist Amiri Baraka dubbed "soulfood" in the 1960s has evolved. Forty years of change has transformed the cuisine from authentically southern into a variant influenced by the curriculum at French and other cooking schools that has been called haute or nouvelle soul food and even southern revival. Fusion recipes, healthier fare, vegetarian, and even vegan versions of traditional dishes are examples of the food's remarkable resilience and its appeal to all kinds of diners. Few white chefs need to be well versed in African American vernacular cooking, but every good chef is assumed to have mastered le métier or French technique in the kitchen. The black chef is seen as a natural heir to vernacular cooking regardless of whether he or she has grown up on the food. With investments and improvements to the restaurant kitchens and dining rooms, African American culinary professionals and the foods they prepare have adapted, too.[7]

African American vernacular cooking has been a generative source for home cooks, entrepreneurs, marketers, and chefs. It was a primary element in the professional cooking narrative of twentieth-century African America, but foods associated with the black Diaspora have greater value in current restaurant trends. Black chefs embrace the style that is contemporary American and reflects the world's influence: Italy, the Caribbean, Asia, France, and Latin America.

Chefs Marvin Woods and Steve Simmons both acknowledge their debt to African American vernacular cooking as a core culinary practice that made it possible to innovate in their professional kitchens. Sweet potatoes, once a regional secret, are now French fried in restaurants, chipped and bagged for retail sale, and aggressively promoted as a healthy side dish. West African and Caribbean-style spicy seasonings flavor appetizers and entrees at mainstream restaurants. Trends and styles may pass between black chefs, traditional African American restaurants, and the mainstream, but eventually they reach similar diners with expectations shaped by the culture and the economy. The difference is simply the point of access where a diner meets a restaurant trend. Early adopters taste an organic lettuce variety at a high-end restaurant, but more people will see it once it reaches the McDonalds salad menu.

Gourmands in black neighborhoods appreciated the taste of jerk chicken long before it was widely available at the local quick service or casual dining restaurant. As food trends travel the racial and cultural boundaries, they can foster professional conversations that inevitably veer toward such substantive topics as culture, history, and identity.

Sweet Potato Pie

1 prepared piecrust	1/4 cup dark brown sugar
3 or 4 medium sweet potatoes, orange or pale yellow	1 tablespoon honey
	Pinch of salt
	Pinch of cayenne
3 tablespoons unsalted butter	1 teaspoon imitation rum flavoring
1/2 teaspoon ground nutmeg	1 1/2 teaspoons vanilla extract
1/2 teaspoon ground cloves	3 large eggs
1 teaspoon ground cinnamon	3/4 cup heavy cream
1/4 cup granulated white sugar	1/4 cup whole milk

(1) Bake sweet potatoes in a 350° F oven for an hour to two hours or until they are soft. After they have cooled, peel and mash the potatoes and measure out 2 cups of potato puree. Save any extra for another dish. (2) To the potato puree mix in the butter, cinnamon, nutmeg, salt, cayenne, and honey until well blended. (3) In another bowl whisk the eggs until blended, add sugars and continue stirring until creamy. (4) Next add the vanilla and imitation rum and mix. End with the milk and cream and continue stirring. Combine the two mixtures and stir until smooth. (5) Pour mix into piecrust and bake in 375° F oven for 40 to 50 minutes—checking regularly. Leftover sweet potato mix can be baked in a buttered dish along with the pie.

The sustainable foods revolution connects notions of American pastoralism, race, class, commerce, and healthy, delicious food and delivers it all to a nearby restaurant table. Chef and cookbook author Edna Lewis's childhood experiences on a Virginia farm are invested with new meaning as a result of the California sustainable foods revolution. Alice Waters, a founder of the Berkeley, California restaurant Chez Panisse, and Lewis shared a commitment to farm-fresh seasonal ingredients, organic when possible, modestly cooked in combinations to highlight the natural flavors. Waters was

Biscuits. Courtesy of the author.

influenced by French culinary traditions and Lewis was influenced by her knowledge of farming and the culinary traditions of the American South. Although they were of different generations, regions, and experiences, they shared the responsibility of advocacy. Lewis was an early and prominent supporter of efforts to preserve southern foodways. Waters's involvement with farmers' markets and healthier school meals reflects the tradition lived by Lewis, her family, and other farmers. Producers of the food she sourced for her restaurant—seasonal, high quality, locally grown—organized themselves into an influential, regional microindustry that inspired other chefs and restaurateurs interested in fusion cooking with locally grown ingredients. Their combined efforts propelled a locally grown, sustainable, food revolution. The foods and the philosophy shaped other California restaurants including Thomas Keller's French Laundry and Deborah Madison's Greens. Govind Armstrong grew up in southern California restaurants on French California cuisine. That sensibility structures his very contemporary cookbook of hors d'oeuvres and small plates, as well as the menus at his Table 8 restaurants in Los Angeles and Miami.[8]

Whether a culinary professional acquires skills and experience through internships or from a degree program, food service, especially in restaurant kitchens, is strenuous work completed over long hours. For black chefs with few peers in stressful restaurant kitchens, the experience can be isolating. Restaurant kitchens are competitive environments where shortcomings and differences can be unpleasantly exploited. Black chefs worry that ideas about race overly affect perceptions of their skills and abilities. A chef who is trained in French or another cuisine meets a potential employer who believes she can only cook collards and fried chicken. Limited opportunities result in professionally trained black chefs who are cooking ribs, fried chicken, and collards with very standard recipes. Food service for school districts or other institutional clients is a reasonable and lucrative alternative to unforgiving restaurant kitchens, but a school district kitchen does not produce stars.

Buttermilk Biscuits

4 1/2 cups unbleached all-purpose flour sifted with a little extra for dusting the cutting board
1 tablespoon baking powder
1 tablespoon sugar
1 teaspoon kosher salt
1/2 teaspoon baking soda
4 tablespoons unsalted butter, cold in chunks
1/3 cup vegetable shortening, ideally trans fat free organic
1 1/3 cups buttermilk

(1) Preheat oven to 450° F. (2) Sift the dry ingredients into a large bowl. Cut in shortening and butter with a pastry cutter, fork, or in a food processor. Slicing into the mixture with two knives moving in opposite directions is another option. When the mix is a coarse powder with little lumps of buttered flour, it is ready. (3) Add buttermilk slowly to the dry mix pouring into the center and stopping to blend. Add the cup and mix the dough from the center and then pull in the edges. The dry mix may be wet enough to become dough with less than the full amount of milk, or it may need a little more. Once it is wet enough to stick together as dough, stop pouring. Dust the sides of the bowl with flour. This should make it easier to collect the dough with your hands by rolling it into the floured sides of the bowl. Turn dough out onto a floured surface and knead with floured hands between five and seven times, being careful not to overknead. Separate the dough into two sections, putting one aside in the bowl and placing the other on the board. Then pat, or roll with rolling pin, the dough out into a half-inch to one-inch thick shape. (4) Pierce the dough all over with a fork dipped in flour to prevent air bubbles, and then use a floured cutter or glass to cut out the biscuits. Cut them as close together as possible to avoid scrap dough and push straight down avoiding the temptation to twist or wiggle

the cutter. Any scrap dough can be added to the second section, which should be patted or rolled out and cut the same way. (5) Place them close together on a heavy, ungreased baking sheet and bake for 10 to 17 minutes, but check how quickly they are cooking. Remove once the tops are brown and crusty.

STAR CHEFS

An early group of African American chefs realized commercial success and celebrity status before the Food Network, blogs, reality TV shows, culinary memoirs, and other new media paved a new path to fame. Edna Lewis at Café Nicholson and Brooklyn's Gage & Tollner, Sylvia Woods through her Harlem restaurant Sylvia's, Mildred Council at Mama Dips Kitchen in Chapel Hill, North Carolina, and Leah Chase of the New Orleans restaurant Dooky Chase were all personally branding their restaurants by the late 1970s. B. Smith founded the restaurant group B. Smith's with locations in New York City and Washington, D.C., soon after. She may be the most familiar representative of a group of pioneering black models and arts figures—Norma Jean Darden, Toukie Smith, Eric V. Copage, and Alexander Smalls—who have leveraged public recognition into culinary and related lifestyle businesses. Delilah Winder reframed B. Smith's outline and opened retail counters at Philadelphia's Reading Terminal market and the Amtrak train station. Calling the venture Delilah's, she served traditional food to hungry travelers and built on that recognition with a restaurant location, catering unit, and a cookbook.

Smothered Chops

1/4 cup all-purpose flour
4 tablespoons Italian seasoned breadcrumbs
3 tablespoons olive oil
1/2 teaspoon ground black
pepper
2 tablespoons chopped
parsley
2 tablespoon minced garlic
1/4 cup cream cheese

1 tablespoon Parmesan
cheese
6 or 8 chops, lamb or pork,
trimmed
2 tablespoons butter, preferably unsalted
1 cup chopped onions
1 cup low-sodium chicken
broth
1 tablespoon balsamic vinegar

(continued)

(1) Mix flour, 3 tablespoons of breadcrumbs, and pepper on a plate for dredging the chops. Drag the chops through the flour and coat both sides. (2) Cook the meat in a pan with the heated oil and one of the tablespoons of garlic. Cook over medium heat until they are done. Remove the chops from the pan and set aside to warm. (3) Add butter, vinegar, 1 tablespoon of parsley, remaining garlic, remaining breadcrumbs, and onions to the cooking pan and cook until they are soft. Slowly pour in chicken broth and simmer. Add cream cheese and stir to blend in lumps and thicken the sauce. Serve chops with sauce and remaining parsley sprinkled over the sauce.

These chefs identified strategies for connecting the success of the restaurant to their own personal appeal and translating that into cookbook sales and product lines that ultimately enhance the restaurant. These women, and they are primarily women, are celebrity culinary figures whose model typifies the star chef ideal. Culinary schools and professional kitchens did not welcome women in the late 1960s and 1970s; some of the most noted women culinary figures including Julia Child made their own way to the professional kitchen. Chase, Woods, and Smith all gained professional experience in their restaurants rather than culinary school or as apprentices in a mentor's kitchen. As the minority, women, African Americans, and Latinos still found that the professional kitchen can be an insensitive and sometimes hostile work environment. The alternative was their own kitchen, and there they created recipes for success. They crafted models to suit their strengths and promoted them nationally. Another generation of black women chefs—Jacqueline Cholmondeley, Deborah Fewell, Reva Bell, and Hannah Sweets have appeared in the food press—has moved from culinary school training to the restaurant kitchen where they may follow an established route or create new ones.

Ironically, the formalization of the celebrity chef circuit has given these well-known chefs periodic publicity, but no new African American super chef has emerged from this public relations machine. Chefs who nurture a career by moving to challenging restaurant jobs, making television appearances, releasing cookbooks, appearing at events, and courting the press may still need the endorsements, national product lines, or casual dining chain restaurant menus that have so far been elusive. Endorsements can be complicated. For many African Americans the food service or cooking brand icon is still too close to the misappropriated images of Cream of Wheat's Rastus, Aunt Jemima, and Uncle Ben. Aunt Jemima and Uncle Ben have undergone frequent makeovers on their public image or of their careers, but memories of their beginnings have been hard to erase. Uncle Ben may have a Web-based executive suite (www.unclebens.com), but he remains a complicated icon.

Community breakfast outside Sylvia's in Harlem to celebrate the restaurant's 40th anniversary. AP Photo/Stuart Ramson.

Unlike those early examples, today's black brand icons—B. Smith, Uncle Wiley, and at one point cookie broker Famous Amos—are well compensated and they maintain full control of the face and name.

Swedish superstar Marcus Samuelsson is the one black chef most food enthusiasts could identify if prompted. He is executive chef at New York's Aquavit, has written several cookbooks, stars in a Discovery Channel television show, has a Starbucks licensing deal, and has consulted on restaurants in other American cities. The late Patrick Clark, a second-generation chef who distinguished himself at New York's Odeon Cafe, Washington, D.C.'s Hay-Adams Hotel, and finally the Tavern on the Green, was an inspirational figure who artfully managed a major New York kitchen, volunteered for charitable causes, and supported other black culinary professionals' careers. His friends say that while he was hospitalized for the congestive heart failure that killed him in 1998, he would duck into the hospital kitchen to prepare meals for fellow patients. Clark is remembered whenever food enthusiasts discuss the situation for black culinary professionals, although the conversation inevitably moves to those who are currently working in restaurants or running their own. In the Northeast Herb Wilson, Ricky Moore, Keith Williams, and Lloyd Roberts have run kitchens in high-profile restaurants.

Washington, D.C., native Timothy Dean saw professional cooking as a child in his grandfather's North Carolina barbecue restaurant. He trained in French kitchens in Washington, D.C., while a student at Howard University. With experience in restaurants on the East and West Coasts, he opened the popular Timothy Dean's at the St. Regis Hotel in Washington, D.C. He now runs Timothy Dean Bistro in Baltimore. Chef Darryl Petty and wine director Brian Duncan are representative of a smaller group of black culinary professionals in the Midwest. Jeff Henderson or Chef Jeff is a former executive chef at the Bellagio Resort, chef de cuisine at Caesars Palace, and a former drug dealer who discovered his passion for cooking while incarcerated. He calls his southern style food cooked with California technique Posh Urban Cuisine, and his memoir *Cooked: From the Streets to the Stove, From Cocaine to Foie Gras* was quickly optioned as a film project.

Pastry chef Warren Brown left a law career to build his Cakelove franchise in metropolitan Washington, D.C. He has published recipes in his book *Cakelove* and is host of the Food Network television show Sugar Rush. Rahman "Chef Rock" Harper graduated from Johnson and Wales University, was executive chef at B. Smith's Washington, D.C., restaurant, is head chef at Terra Verde Green Valley Ranch Resort, and was a winner of Gordon Ramsay's Fox reality show Hell's Kitchen. With East and West Coast restaurants, a stylishly current cookbook, and appearances as a reality TV judge, Govind Armstrong will become a more familiar presence, too. Supported by a restaurant group, book publisher, and his own telegenic appeal, Armstrong is ready to join or surpass other high-profile chefs.

Identification as chef is a milestone. Some distinguish between cooks and chefs who run kitchen and restaurant, but increasingly black leaders are found across the industry from conservative commentator Herman Cain, the former chairman of Godfather's Pizza and past president of the National Restaurant Association to wine sommelier and distributor André Mack. The number of black students at culinary schools is still a small percentage of the student enrollment, but the opportunities available to them will encourage other budding black chefs to consider culinary school options. The percentage of managers in the industry is growing as well, and although there are few black star chefs, plenty of black chefs have found their own routes to greater recognition via regional and national media. A high-profile national endorsement is the next pinnacle and it is sure to come soon.

NOTES

1. Lena Williams, "Preparing Soul Food Can Now Be as Easy as Opening a Can," *The New York Times*, May 26, 1993.

2. Todd Hale, Patricia McDonough, and Patricia Andrews-Keenan, "The African-American Consumer: Is the Cultural Divide Breaking Down?" *Consumer Insight Magazine* 4 (September 2007).

3. Kameshwari Pothukuchi, "Attracting Supermarkets to Inner-City Neighborhoods: Economic Development Outside the Box," *Economic Development Quarterly* 19 (2005); Kameshwari Pothukuchi, *Attracting Grocery Retail Investment to Inner-City Neighborhoods: Planning Outside the Box* (Detroit: Wayne State University Press, 2000); James Johnson-Piett with Duane Perry, Hannah Burton, and David Adler, *Food For Every Child: The Need for More Supermarkets in Philadelphia* (Philadelphia: The Food Trust, 2001), http://www.thefoodtrust.org/pdf/supermar.pdf; Allison Karpyn and Francine Axler, *Food Geography: How Food Access Affects Diet and Health* (Philadelphia: The Food Trust, 2006); R. W. Cotterill and A. W. Franklin, *The Urban Grocery Store Gap.* Food Marketing Policy Issue Paper No. 8 (Storrs, CT: Food Marketing Policy Center, University of Connecticut, 1995); S. Zenk, A. Schulz, T. Hollis-Neely, R. Campbell, N. Holmes, G. Watkins, R. Nwankwo, and A. Odoms-Young "Fruit and Vegetable Intake in African Americans: Income and Store Characteristics," *American Journal of Preventive Medicine* 29 (2005): 1–9.

4. Mark Winne, *Closing the Food Gap: Resetting the Table in the Land of Plenty* (Boston: Beacon Press, 2008); Tracie McMillan, "Urban Farmers' Crops Go From Vacant Lot to Market," *The New York Times*, Wednesday, May 7, 2008; Rebecca Solnit, "Detroit Arcadia: Exploring the Post-Modern Landscape," *Harper's Magazine*, July 2007, 65–73; Amanda Shaffer, *The Persistence of L.A.'s Grocery Gap: The Need for a New Food Policy and Approach to Market Development* (Los Angeles: Urban Environmental Policy Institute, Occidental College, 2002); Eric Sloss and Jonathan Potts, "Students' Plan for Hill District Grocery Store Wins JP Morgan National Competition," *Carnegie Mellon Today.com* 2, no. 2 (August 2005).

5. Marjorie L. DeVault, *Feeding the Family: The Social Organization of Caring as Gendered Work* (Chicago: The University of Chicago Press, 1991); Micaela di Leonardo, "The Female World of Cards and Holidays: Women, Families, and the Work of Kinship," *Signs* 12, no. 3 (Spring, 1987): 440–453; Marvalene H. Hughes, "Soul, Black Women, and Food," in *Food and Culture: A Reader*, ed. Carole Counihan and Penny Van Esterik (New York: Routledge, 1997); Bebe Moore Campbell, *Sweet Summer: Growing Up With and Without My Dad* (New York: Ballantine Books, 1989); Sherrie A. Inness, ed., *Cooking Lessons: The Politics of Gender and Food* (Lanham, MD: Rowman & Littlefield Publishers, 2001).

6. Robin L. Jarrett, Kevin M. Roy, and Linda Burton, "Fathers in the 'Hood': Insights from Qualitative Research on Low-Income African-American Men," in *Handbook of Father Involvement: Multidisciplinary Perspectives*, ed. Catherine S. Tamis-LeMonda and Natasha Cabrera (Mahwah, NJ: Lawrence Erlbaum Associates, 2002); K. Kofi Moyo, *Real Men Cook: Rites, Rituals, and Recipes for Living* (New York: Fireside, 2005); K. Kofi Moyo and Barack Obama, *Real Men Cook: More Than 100 Easy Recipes Celebrating Tradition and Family* (New York: Fireside, 2006).

7. Amiri Baraka, "Soul Food," in *Home: Social Essays* (New York: William Morrow, 1966); Warren Belasco, *Appetite for Change: How the Counterculture Took on the Food Industry, 1966–1988* (New York: Pantheon, 1989); Kimberly D. Nettles, "'Saving' Soul Food," *Gastronomica* 7, no. 3 (2007): 106–113.

8. David Kamp, *The United States of Arugula: How We Became a Gourmet Nation* (New York: Broadway Books, 2006); Govind Armstrong, *Small Bites, Big Nights: Seductive Little Plates for Intimate Occasions and Lavish Parties* (New York: Clarkson Potter, 2007); Florence Fabricant, "For Blacks, Chef Jobs Finally Call," *The New York Times*, October 20, 1993; Michael Ruhlman, "Black Chefs Struggle for the Top," *The New York Times*, April 5, 2006.

BIBLIOGRAPHY

Andreyeva, Tatiana, Daniel M. Blumenthal, Marlene B. Schwartz, Michael W. Long, and Kelly D. Brownell. "Availability and Prices of Foods Across Stores and Neighborhoods: The Case of New Haven, Connecticut," *Health Affairs* 27 no. 5 (September / October 2008): 1381–1388.

Armstrong, Govind. *Small Bites, Big Nights: Seductive Little Plates for Intimate Occasions and Lavish Parties*. New York: Clarkson Potter, 2007.

Baraka, Amiri. "Soul Food." In *Home: Social Essays*. New York: William Morrow, 1966.

Belasco, Warren. *Appetite for Change: How the Counterculture Took on the Food Industry. 1966–1988*. New York: Pantheon, 1989.

Campbell, Bebe Moore. *Sweet Summer: Growing Up With and Without My Dad*. New York: Ballantine Books, 1989.

Cotterill, Ronald W., and Andrew W. Franklin. *The Urban Grocery Store Gap*. Food Marketing Policy Issue Paper No. 8, Storrs, CT: Food Marketing Policy Center, University of Connecticut, 1995.

DeVault, Marjorie L. *Feeding the Family: The Social Organization of Caring as Gendered Work*. Chicago: The University of Chicago Press, 1991.

Friedman, Roberta R. "Access to Healthy Foods in Low-Income Neighborhoods," In *Opportunities for Public Policy*. New Haven, CT: Rudd Center for Food Policy and Obesity, Yale University, Fall 2008.

Hale, Todd, Patricia McDonough, and Patricia Andrews-Keenan. "The African-American Consumer: Is the Cultural Divide Breaking Down?" *Consumer Insight Magazine* 4 (September 2007).

Hughes, Marvalene H. "Soul, Black Women, and Food." In *Food and Culture: A Reader*. ed. Carole Counihan and Penny Van Esterik. New York: Routledge, 1997.

Inness, Sherrie A., ed. *Cooking Lessons: The Politics of Gender and Food*. Lanham, MD: Rowman & Littlefield Publishers, 2001.

Jarrett, Robin L., Kevin M. Roy, and Linda Burton. "Fathers in the 'Hood': Insights from Qualitative Research on Low-Income African-American Men." In *Handbook of Father Involvement: Multidisciplinary Perspectives*, ed. Catherine S. Tamis-LeMonda and Natasha Cabrera. Mahwah, NJ: Lawrence Erlbaum Associates, 2002.

Johnson-Piett, James with Duane Perry, Hannah Burton, and David Adler, *Food for Every Child: The Need for More Supermarkets in Philadelphia*. Philadelphia: The Food Trust, 2001, http://www.thefoodtrust.org/pdf/supermar.pdf.

Karpyn, Allison, and Francine Axler. *Food Geography: How Food Access Affects Diet and Health*. Philadelphia: The Food Trust, 2006.

Moyo, K. Kofi. *Real Men Cook: Rites, Rituals, and Recipes for Living*. New York: Fireside, 2005.

Moyo, K. Kofi, and Barack Obama. *Real Men Cook: More Than 100 Easy Recipes Celebrating Tradition and Family*. New York: Fireside, 2006.

Nettles, Kimberly D. "'Saving' Soul Food." *Gastronomica* 7, no. 3(2007): 106–113.

Pothukuchi, Kameshwari. *Attracting Grocery Retail Investment to Inner-City Neighborhoods: Planning Outside the Box*. Detroit: Wayne State University Press, 2000.

Shaffer, Amanda. *The Persistence of L.A.'s Grocery Gap: The Need for a New Food Policy and Approach to Market Development*. Los Angeles: Urban Environmental Policy Institute, Occidental College, 2002.

Solnit, Rebecca. "Detroit Arcadia: Exploring the Post-Modern Landscape." *Harper's Magazine*, July 2007, 65–73.

Williams, Lena. "Preparing Soul Food Can Now Be as Easy as Opening a Can." *The New York Times*, May 26, 1993.

Winne, Mark. *Closing the Food Gap: Resetting the Table in the Land of Plenty*. Boston: Beacon Press, 2008.

4

Typical Meals

A large segment of the African American population is conservative regarding food. Like others, black Americans expect three meals a day and assume that schedule ensures a balanced diet. Diet fads and culinary trends go in and out of style, but African Americans have been skeptical of food trends and whimsical fads related to eating. The three-meals-a-day regimen is a trusted meal schedule even when time, money, and creativity make meal preparation harder than it should be. A weekday breakfast is part of a school or work routine, so it is ideally quick, convenient, and satisfying. The lunch break has gradually evolved from an important family meal to a critical personal hour where students and working professionals affirm individual identity through a meal. During the workday, lunch hour is an important respite. The actual meal, possibly the day's most daring food choice, and the hour allotted to it are savored. Depending on the work environment, lunch is a time for colleagues to share stories with friends while enjoying a meal that someone else prepares.

Many public schools serve breakfast and lunch, which simplifies meal planning and minimizes a potential instructional barrier for young learners. During the short lunch period, students conduct the necessary identity work that goes along with nutrition. Dinner, potentially the most relaxed meal of the day, allows for a culturally or ethnically distinct dining experience. But for most busy individuals, a weeknight dinner will be a meal that is easily and quickly prepared. Young professionals are more likely to invest time to prepare a special dinner for friends or to mark an occasion. Working people with children identify dinner as a family meal, but competing school activities, the responsibilities of a longer workday, and popular culture have diminished the sanctity of the dinner hour. Continued innovation in the packaged food industry has made it easier to prepare convenient, inexpensive, flexible dinners to accommodate busy schedules. Further growth in convenience foods may discourage some from cooking meals from scratch, but research data suggest that African Americans and Latinos persist in spending more time on cooking.

MORE THAN A MEAL

Making decisions about meals was one of the first freedoms that African Americans could exercise. Those who kept a small garden during slavery could choose to supplement their diet or their income with the produce. Even when a three-meal-a-day regimen was not an option, blacks knew that prosperous free Americans had three meals. The journey toward financial stability can be understood through meal changes.[1]

African Americans who farmed in the late nineteenth-century South assumed responsibility for providing their own food after generations of receiving basic provisions under slavery. Some sharecroppers, hired by white landowners to continue working on land they farmed during slavery, farmed on close margins never making a profit. Growing or earning enough for a varied and nutritious diet was never easy for sharecropping families. In areas where black families farmed land they owned, residents could reach a level of financial independence. Early diet studies run by U.S. Department of Agriculture researchers found evidence of a more varied and nutritious diet in communities where blacks farmed their own land. A well-prepared, substantial mid-day meal was an important indicator of a family's success and the community's progress. These symbolic changes in African American dining habits of the late nineteenth century had national implications.[2]

African Americans understood the early twentieth century through political groups, social clubs, service organizations, settlement houses, churches, and philosopher-activists committed to racial improvement. Booker T. Washington and W.E.B. Du Bois were the most widely recognized intellectual leaders of the period, but they had competition. Their priorities were economic and political, but they influenced African American life to the level of daily meals. Both recognized salvation in the idea of a New Negro who would radically reform white Americans' ideas about African American citizens. Critics questioned the effort to cultivate Victorian sensibilities in black Americans, but Du Bois and Washington dreamed of a more ambitious project. They hoped to revitalize the domestic sphere to assist with the resurrection of African America. A network of rural primary schools, black colleges, churches, social clubs, and business groups advanced an agenda that valued the pursuit of middle-class family norms. Middle-class black women formed social clubs that modeled appropriate behavior for their less privileged sisters, as they exemplified the social progress blacks had achieved in the final years of the nineteenth century. Recasting black women as American mothers, wives, and ladies was a critical piece of the New Negro campaign. Essays and articles published by Booker T. Washington, Rev. W.E.C. Wright, Fannie B. Williams, and N. B. Wood among others pushed the term *New Negro* into a cultural dialogue that culminated in Alain Locke's 1925 anthology *The New Negro*. New Negroes, educated, urbane, and financially stable, embraced the norms of contemporary American dining. Their community organizations and educational centers offered instructional programs to educate new migrants from the rural South on nutrition and diet. Black migrants from the rural South had a head start on the European immigrants who would become the target population of reformers' Americanization efforts. An arsenal of incentives from settlement house cooking lessons to the G. I. Bill fortified that campaign. It successfully standardized American dining hours and created the context for a common national culinary culture in the packaged foods that soldiers ate and the shared experience of civilian rationing during World War II.[3]

BREAKFAST

Other meals are revised and debated, but breakfast is the meal with the most impact for the day. Eating breakfast affects weight gain, increases energy, and improves performance, although it is an underappreciated meal and likely to be eaten in transit. Coffee, instant, percolator, drip, or takeout, is a basic and tea, black or herbal, is a less popular morning beverage alternative. The proliferation of coffee and donut chains along with quick service restaurant breakfasts has made mobile breakfast an option for commuters who race to work in their own cars or on public transportation. A quick breakfast at home can be a toaster pastry or microwave pancakes, hot or cold breakfast cereal, or a modified full breakfast with eggs, toast, and juice. Because it is one of the meals served at school, students have the choice of a morning meal that is balanced according to the U.S. Department of Agriculture to include fruit or fruit juice, milk, cereal, or a breakfast carbohydrate. Weekday mornings have a purpose and Sunday morning is reserved for church, which leaves Saturday for a more leisurely breakfast. The impulse that leads to investing the time to cook a big breakfast may be the most significant aspect of the meal.[4]

LUNCH

Lunch can be the shortest and most flexible meal of the day. Breakfast boosters reasserted its centrality while lunch moved out to the margin. It is the meal usually scheduled between 12:00 P.M. and 1:30 P.M. and often skipped, worked through, or filled with other obligations. Lunch can be easy to miss at work, but it is a school requirement. To accommodate overscheduled school days, however, the first lunch period can begin as early as 10:30 A.M. During lunch, workers conduct business, students finish homework, and some take their lunch to enjoy a meal.

School Lunch

President Harry S. Truman's 1946 National School Lunch Act was meant to guarantee that young Americans received proper nutrition. Creation of this World War II era federal policy followed years of school-based nutritional programs administered by school districts in cities across the nation. The National School Lunch Act brought federal standards to programs already in existence in America's cities and rural areas. Today free and subsidized lunches feed 30.6 million children whose families qualify based on income and national poverty level indices. Nutritional standards mandate that the lunches served at school offer a third of the Recommended Dietary Allowances of vitamin A, iron, calcium, protein, vitamin C, and calories. Breakfast should provide one-fourth of the calories and recommended dietary allowances. Food service managers choose meals based on taste and cost, but they must monitor fat levels, sodium, cholesterol, and find ways to include as many grains, vegetables, and fruits as possible.

School lunch and the quality of food available in school are topics of interest affecting rural school districts and urban. Parents, school administrators, taxpayers, farmers, and natural foods enthusiasts are questioning the decisions about food served at school in local and national campaigns. They are emphasizing the health, cultural, and environmental benefits of conscientious and sustainable school lunch programs. Berkeley, California restaurateur Alice Waters partnered with the neighboring Martin Luther King Jr. Middle School to develop the Edible Schoolyard. The flagship in the Rethinking School Lunch effort, the Edible Schoolyard gives urban students the experience of growing, harvesting, and preparing seasonal produce on a one-acre organic garden. A curriculum component makes it possible for other schools to adopt the model and Waters expects to see that happen. She brought the fight to Capitol Hill where she lobbied Congress in ways that included bringing a wood burning pizza oven to the National Mall to serve legislators a healthy lunch.

Waters's efforts targeted Congress, but her program, increased interest, and rigorous analysis of the food in schools have influenced local districts. Continued evaluation of school lunch and school food policies has led school systems across the country to eliminate soft drink vending machines, candy

Healthful lunch for New York City charter school students. AP Photo/Mary Altaffer.

sales, sugary birthday treats, and other foods in conflict with healthier eating. Financial incentives reward districts that source locally grown produce and serve it in school lunches through the Small Farms/School Meals Initiative or Farm-to-School. A typical middle school lunch menu might include a beef taco and nacho chips, chicken stir fry with brown rice, a fruit cup, and milk. Lunch one afternoon at a high school might be macaroni and cheese or meatloaf and gravy with carrots. Milk, fruit, salads, and sandwiches would be available, too. The politics of school lunch are not limited to the quality of the food or the nutritional value. Identity, economic and social status, and popular culture are on display in the school cafeteria.

Children bring lunch that is a known quantity to school, but the lunch line promises variety and surprise, and the student can exit with a nutritious, hot meal. Subsidized lunches make the nutritious, hot meal a reality for all students. Younger children take their lunch, even the subsidized, eagerly, but middle and high school students understand that the cost of a free meal might be charged to their reputation. The organization of some lunch lines reveals to students which of their peers are recipients of free or subsidized lunch. That revelation can highlight uncomfortable economic differences. Choosing to skip the lunch line preserves social standing at the expense of a necessary meal. As districts reevaluate food programs some are also exploring cafeteria line technology to keep all students' financial data private. Another form of school lunch anxiety annoys middle-class black students who attend integrated schools where they are an identifiable minority of the student body. Black students seated at the same table in a cafeteria of white students appear to have segregated themselves at the "black table," although in fact they simply choose to sit with friends, as adjoining tables of white students had. The black lunch table erupts as a rancorous topic of debate intermittently, although it is no more controversial than the tables of athletes, choir members, actors, or friends from a neighborhood or elementary school. For teens lunch hour is a valuable time for establishing and managing relationships while eating a meal.[5]

Lunch at Work

The lunch hour is an ideal time for running errands, eating takeout and catching up on work, or heading out to exercise. Once the decision to eat lunch has been made, there is still plenty to choose. Enjoying a lunch break during the workday is heavily dependent on the character of the work environment, the employee's position, and the surrounding neighborhood. Large corporations, public institutions, and even universities reward workers with cafeterias designed to resemble the food courts in shopping malls. With salad bars, grill stations, sandwich lines, and a hot entrée area, diners can choose from an impressive array of menu choices. At these large corporations lunch may be subsidized and staff suggestions or feedback solicited.

At a small business, the size of the staff and the responsibilities of the position define how lunch is taken. The presence of colleagues who are diverse in age, ethnicity, and culture and assignments that are creative and interesting or tedious and exhausting can also influence the lunch experience. In a work environment that feels foreign and oppressive, lunch is a welcome respite that is anxiously guarded. At a culturally sensitive environment, a social service organization, arts institution, or a barbershop, lunch may be communal or even family-style and celebratory. Because weekday lunch is a meal without family obligations, it is a time for indulgence for some at work. With a full group of dining choices and a few that are unique ethnic restaurants, an employee lunch break is a chance to try red snapper or oxtails from a Jamaican restaurant, a chicken dish from a Chinese takeout, a specialty sandwich, or a meal of African American heritage favorites. Lunch out with colleagues from different backgrounds is another opportunity to gain a new perspective or discover new foods. For those who are beginning careers or making a major transition, lunch is a critical part of an orientation to the new environment. Forty years ago legislation, legal rulings, and presidential orders forced more equality into the American economy, but comfortably, diverse environments remain rare exceptions. As American workers negotiate cultural and racial differences in public spheres, a shared lunch during the day reinforces the lessons learned on company time.[6]

DINNER

Preparing dinner after an exhausting day can be an enjoyably, restorative time of sharing the day's stories while finishing the tasks necessary to complete the meal. It can just as easily become another assignment in an exhausting day. Whether making dinner is a source of inspiration or frustration, for busy African American families it is the day's one meal that comfortably accommodates distinctive culinary traditions. Unlike breakfast at a quick service restaurant or a cafeteria lunch, the person who does the cooking will make all the decisions about a dinner prepared at home. On average Americans eat 4.9 dinners at home a week and 40 percent of those are prepared meals or frozen dinners. Recipes or preparations that require stovetop cooking or roasting are preferred. Grilling, pan sautéing, and using the microwave speed meal preparation along, too. Almost half of all dinners cooked at home are ready to eat in 30 minutes, although African American consumers on average purchase more foods that require multistep preparation. Speed and convenience are essential elements of the successful family dinner on a weeknight.

Preparing the hurried dinner is the time when innate cooking impulses are expressed. If the meal comes together without a recipe and the cooking is improvised, dinner is a success if the result approximates a mix of familiar flavors, a complex sweet, salty, tangy taste that emerges after hours of cooking. The meal can be the product of simple preparation techniques familiar to anyone cooking in America, or it can be loosely based on rules from African American heritage cooking. A dinner of chicken or salmon served with canned or frozen green beans and macaroni, rice, or potatoes can be cooked to resemble a dinner at any home or accented to reflect African American culinary history.

This is a quickly prepared, basic dinner improved on by the universal impulse to add flavor to the food. The choice of seasoning and the flavor pursued align the meal with African American vernacular cooking. The chicken or salmon is seasoned with a spice mix, preferably one of the low sodium varieties but one with traces of heat and salt. For a healthier and faster dinner, the poultry or fish could be broiled, grilled, or given another layer of flavor with the application of a breadcrumb coating and oven-frying rather than broiling. The green beans are flavored with a small piece of lean, smoked meat, and balanced with vinegar and black pepper. Another side dish of macaroni, rice, potatoes, carrots, or corn is cooked plainly for speed, although the natural sugars of the carrots or corn might be enhanced. These choices would be instinctive and the result of time spent in the kitchen observing others. Experience and observation are ultimately as helpful as recipes in training a cook to gauge how to achieve the proper or familiar taste in a dish so that it will please others. These improvised or loosely planned meals were familiar routines, but they are now modeled for beginning cooks by established chefs on television, radio, and in print. A well-known chef takes a journalist shopping at a farmers' market and cooks a meal from whatever produce they happen to find at market. The meal is delicious, the journalist is delighted and impressed, and the chef's current project is favorably mentioned. In print this seems daunting, but actually every day people spontaneously decide on the evening's dinner based on what they find fresh at the grocery store. Instincts or reflexes sharpened by observation and practice guide them in cooking a meal without recipes. For many black cooks the skill set is based on lessons learned from the preparation of recipes that belong to African American heritage cuisine.[7]

WEEKEND MEALS AND SUNDAY DINNER

Weekends are associated with leisure, but the short break can be as hectic as a weekday. Between family household chores and frequent youth activities weekends can become very scheduled. Even if Saturday morning offers no real relaxation, there may still be a yearning to sleep late and savor a big breakfast. A Saturday morning breakfast menu must include simmered grits or fried hash browns, cornbread or biscuits, and sausage, bacon, or another breakfast meat. Fresh-caught and fried fish could be served at breakfast, too. There would be eggs and possibly pancakes with fruit, special syrups or jellies, and coffee, juice, and milk. An indulgent weekend breakfast is at odds with the way many family's lives are ordered, but the idea is appealing and the meal carries the satisfaction of an acknowledged tradition. Many of these foods are packaged and frozen or processed for instant cooking, so the sentiment of a big family breakfast can be quickly and easily realized.

Singles and couples without children make an event of the Saturday brunch—or a long morning coffee—at home, a coffee shop, or a restaurant. Restaurants in major cities have cultivated a brunch crowd, and the secular Saturday brunch can be repackaged for Sunday. Restaurants in New York City's Harlem and some other historic black neighborhoods developed a post-worship, Sunday brunch experience that is particularly appealing for tourists. Idiosyncratic jazz and gospel brunch events at small independent restaurants now compete with the House of Blues, casual-dining chains, and personality or theme restaurants that serve a buffet brunch and showcase live musical performances with jazz musicians or gospel choirs. These are special-occasion meals and the foods served are glamorous versions of traditional favorites. The buffet line has scrambled eggs, a waffle station, sweet potato casserole, macaroni and cheese, collard greens, sausage, bacon, chicken in a sauce, fried fish, grits, mixed green salad, buttermilk biscuits, cornbread, fresh fruit, pound cake, fruit cobbler, and pie. Although the jazz brunch may appeal to tourists and visitors, the gospel brunch targets church-going African Americans who could accept worship extending into a meal with gospel music but would not rush to a meal with another kind of music. Gospel or jazz brunches can be terrific meals, but they are scheduled in conflict with Sunday worship.

A hearty brunch in the late morning or early afternoon is followed by a light evening meal later in the day. Supper is an occasion to share heritage recipes for special breakfast foods, quirky sandwiches, and even regional specialties. The best suppers are the result of creative redistribution of components from an earlier meal. Parts of a big Saturday breakfast might reappear as cornbread, fried, reheated, or enhanced with syrup or dairy, or grits embellished with salmon and cheese and baked. Eggs and grilled baloney complete the supper. Improvised leftovers, in this case with a breakfast theme, are prototypical soulfood.

Baked Salmon Grits

2 cups grits, preferably stone-ground, regular is fine, not quick grits
4 cups water
4 cups whole milk
4 tablespoons unsalted butter
1/4 cup Parmesan cheese and a tablespoon of cheese

1/2 cup low-fat mozzarella cheese
1/2 cup light cream
2 large eggs, beaten
1 teaspoon kosher salt
1/2 teaspoon black pepper
1/2 cup cooked or cured salmon, smoked, canned, or grilled and leftover

Preheat oven to 350° F.

(1) Combine the milk and water in a saucepan, cover, and turn the heat to medium until the liquid is nearly boiling. If grits need to be cleaned, rinse them with water and let them sit in a bowl of water. Scoop away any matter that floats to the surface. The grits can be drained in a fine sieve (they are very tiny) and then added to the milk and water with the salt. (2) Reduce the heat to low, remove the top, stir regularly (possibly replacing the top) until the grits are thick and soupy but not watery. Depending on the grits this could take more or less than 40 minutes. (3) Once grits are cooked and have cooled transfer them to a large baking dish. Mix in the other ingredients, reserving the tablespoon of Parmesan. Sprinkle remaining cheese on top of the grits and bake for 30 minutes or until the top forms a crust.

Collard Greens

2 pounds fresh collard greens	1/4 cup apple cider
1 medium onion chopped	1 cup water
4 cloves garlic minced	3 tablespoons olive oil
2 tablespoons black olives in oil, chopped	Salt, freshly ground pepper, vinegar, and hot sauce to
1/4 cup fresh ginger chopped	taste

(1) Wash the greens thoroughly to remove any dirt or pebbles. Cut out any yellow or brown spots on the leaves. Remove the thick center rib and chop or tear the leaves into bite-sized pieces. (2) In a large pot heat the olive oil over a low fire. Once the oil is hot add the onions, garlic, ginger, and olives. Sauté the onion mix, stirring constantly until soft and then pour in the apple cider. (3) Add the greens to the pot followed by the water and reduce the flame. Cover and cook over low heat until the greens are tender. Flavor to taste with salt, pepper, vinegar, and hot sauce.

The welcome table is a metaphor from the Negro spirituals that enslaved Africans created during slavery. In this song the singer promises to eat at the welcome table with Jesus one day. A century after the end of slavery, the song became an anthem of the modern Civil Rights movement when students fought segregated facilities with lunch counter sit-in protests. That generation of singers insisted on sitting at the welcome table where they would feast on equality. The student protesters elegantly linked their freedom fight to those their ancestors imagined while connecting the meal of spiritual salvation to the very tangible meal that segregation denied. Today the phrase is evocative of African American heritage cooking—Jessica Harris and Maya Angelou both have welcome table cookbooks—and memoirs of activists from the political struggles of the modern Civil Rights era. Almost as elegantly, they have redefined the spiritual and corporeal relationship to the symbolic meal inspiriting both recipes and memories.

The food is historically and spiritually significant both for the contexts in which it has already nourished and for the promise of a future meal that reunites. In that way it has become a totally resonant and appropriate metaphor for the meal families and friends share after Sunday church services. This is not just a meal; it is central to the notion of fellowship even as it moves beyond the church walls. The welcome table captures experiences that unite friends, family, worshipers, and guests in a meal that affirms history and relationships through symbolic foods and tastes. This regular, if not weekly, reaffirmation of foodways reintroduces community ideals and history as competing forces threaten their continuity. Holidays can isolate customs and practices, but weekly meals incorporate daily changes, making it possible to believe in that reunion at the welcome table.

NOTES

1. Harvey Levenstein, *Revolution at the Table: The Transformation of the American Diet* (New York: Oxford University Press, 1988); Harvey Levenstein, *Paradox of Plenty: A Social History of Eating in Modern America* (New York: Oxford University Press, 1993).

2. Robert T. Dirks and Nancy Duran, "African American Dietary Patterns at the Beginning of the 20th Century," *The Journal of Nutrition* 131, no. 7 (2001): 1881–1889.

3. Henry Louis Gates Jr., "The Trope of a New Negro and the Reconstruction of the Image of the Black," *Representations, Special Issue: America Reconstructed, 1840–1940* 24 (Autumn, 1988), 129–155; Henry Louis Gates Jr., and Gene Andrew Jarrett, eds. *The New Negro: Readings on Race, Representation, and African American Culture, 1892–1938* (Princeton, NJ: Princeton University Press, 2007).

4. S. G. Affenito, D. R. Thompson, B. A. Barton, D. L. Franko, S. R. Daniels, O. Obarzanek, G. B. Schreiber, and R. H. Striegel-Moore. "Breakfast Consumption by African-American and White Adolescent Girls Correlates Positively with Calcium and Fiber Intake and Negatively with Body Mass Index," *Journal of the American Dietetic Association* 105, no. 6 (2005): 938–945; A. E. Sampson, S. Dixit, A. F. Meyers, and R. Houser Jr., "The Nutritional Impact of Breakfast Consumption on the Diets of Inner-City African-American Elementary School Children," *Journal of the National Medical Association* 87, no. 3 (1995): 195–202; Anna Maria Siega-Riz, Barry M. Popkin, and Terri Carson, "Differences in Food Patterns at Breakfast by Sociodemographic Characteristics among a Nationally Representative Sample of Adults in the United States," *Preventive Medicine* 30, no. 5 (2000): 415–424.

5. Beverly Daniel Tatum, *"Why Are All the Black Kids Sitting Together in the Cafeteria?" and Other Conversations About Race* (New York: Basic Books, 1997); David Kamp, *The United States of Arugula: How We Became a Gourmet Nation* (New York: Broadway Books, 2006); M. Meyer and M. Conklin, "Variables Affecting High School Students Perceptions of School Foodservice," *Journal of the American Dietetic Association* 98, no. 2 (1998): 1424–1431; Carol Pogash, "Free School Lunch Isn't Cool, So Some Students Go Hungry," *The New York Times*, March 1, 2008; Amy Stuart Wells and Robert L. Crain, *Stepping Over the Color Line: African-American Students in White Suburban Schools* (New Haven, CT: Yale University Press, 1997); Constance Newman and Katherine Ralston, *Profiles of Participants in the National School Lunch Program: Data From Two National Surveys,* USDA Economic Research Service Economic Information Bulletin Number 17, August 2006.

6. Reuben A. Buford May, *Talking at Trena's: Everyday Conversations at an African American Tavern* (New York: New York University Press, 2001); Mary Pattillo-McCoy,

Black Picket Fences: Privilege and Peril Among the Black Middle Class (Chicago: University of Chicago Press, 2000).

7. Vertamae Smart-Grosvenor, *Vibration Cooking of the Travel Notes of a Geechee Girl* (New York: Ballantine, 1970).

BIBLIOGRAPHY

Affenito, S. G., D. R. Thompson, B. A. Barton, D. L. Franko, S. R. Daniels, O. Obarzanek, G. B. Schreiber, and R. H. Striegel-Moore. "Breakfast Consumption by African-American and White Adolescent Girls Correlates Positively with Calcium and Fiber Intake and Negatively with Body Mass Index." *Journal of the American Dietetic Association* 105, no. 6 (2005): 938–945.

Dirks, Robert T. and Nancy Duran. "African American Dietary Patterns at the Beginning of the 20th Century." *The Journal of Nutrition* 131, no. 7 (2001): 1881–1889.

Gates, Jr., Henry Louis. "The Trope of a New Negro and the Reconstruction of the Image of the Black." *Representations, Special Issue: America Reconstructed, 1840–1940* 24 (Autumn, 1988): 129–155.

Levenstein, Harvey. *Paradox of Plenty: A Social History of Eating in Modern America.* New York: Oxford University Press, 1993.

May, Reuben A. Buford. *Talking at Trena's: Everyday Conversations at an African American Tavern.* New York: New York University Press, 2001.

Meyer, M. and M. Conklin. "Variables Affecting High School Students Perceptions of School Foodservice." *Journal of the American Dietetic Association* 98, no. 2 (1998): 1424–1431.

Pogash, Carol. "Free School Lunch Isn't Cool, So Some Students Go Hungry." *The New York Times*, March 1, 2008.

Sampson, A. E., S. Dixit, A. F. Meyers, and R. Houser Jr. "The Nutritional Impact of Breakfast Consumption on the Diets of Inner-City African-American Elementary School Children." *Journal of the National Medical Association* 87, no. 3 (1995): 195–202.

Siega-Riz, Anna Maria, Barry M. Popkin, and Terri Carson. "Differences in Food Patterns at Breakfast by Sociodemographic Characteristics among a Nationally Representative Sample of Adults in the United States." *Preventive Medicine* 30, no. 5 (2000): 415–424.

Tatum, Beverly Daniel. *"Why Are All the Black Kids Sitting Together in the Cafeteria?" and Other Conversations About Race.* New York: Basic Books, 1997.

Wells, Amy Stuart, and Robert L. Crain. *Stepping Over the Color Line: African-American Students in White Suburban Schools.* New Haven, CT: Yale University Press, 1997.

5

Eating Out

Conflicting schedules, discriminating palates, and seductive advertising make eating out an incredibly attractive option for many busy African American families, aware young people, and even those whose time and finances should lead them to see home cooking as the logically frugal choice. Growth in the restaurant industry meant that Americans ate 80 restaurant meals per person in 2005. The average American may eat three-fourths of his or her meals at home, but the preference for takeout food is catching up to the stalwart home cook whose meals are made from scratch. Growth at various levels of the restaurant category, greater economic freedom, and some African Americans' more cosmopolitan dining expectations have all helped to increase the frequency of blacks dining out. A meal out can be a regular social arrangement, a special cultural affirmation, a break from the routine for the cook, or an opportunity to enjoy foods not served at home.

The good news for the industry is that more Americans are eating meals outside the home. This is also good news for black America. In restaurants it is still possible for someone with modest skills and big dreams to succeed. Foodservice is the fourth most profitable business category in the 2007 Black Enterprise 100 compilation of black businesses, but there is a caveat. Restaurants have been the theaters where some of the most urgent racial dramas of the late twentieth have been mounted.[1]

African American college students launched their fight for freedom at a North Carolina Woolworth's lunch counter in 1960. Their campaign to end segregated hospitality led to a national student civil rights organization and eventually drew their parents, their peers at other universities, and sympathetic

Sit-in at Woolworth's, Atlanta, October 20, 1960. AP Photo/Horace Cort.

citizens into the civil rights struggle. They succeeded in desegregating public facilities, but some fighting with restaurants for equality continues.

Not many nationally recognized casual dining chains operate restaurants in historically black neighborhoods, but in those areas that have experienced increased restaurant activity, the neighbors associate it with imminent gentrification and the ultimate loss of the area. The success of those new restaurants may be a signal that invites new economic investment as well as municipal and corporate attention to areas that desperately need it. That attention inevitably influences the neighborhood with changes that disproportionately affect the most vulnerable residents and businesses with the longest neighborhood history. But that is not always the case. On Washington D.C.'s U Street corridor, Mahaboob Ben Ali and fiancée Virginia Rollins opened Ben's Chili Bowl in August 1958. The corridor, a "Black Broadway," was the entertainment and arts district that served the historically black institution of higher learning, Howard University. Economic and political realities had an impact on the neighborhood, and the Alis continued serving chili, spicy hot dogs (half smokes), milkshakes, and now turkey and veggie burgers through riots, a stalled economy, the drug wars, and the recent construction boom that has remade U Street.

Ben's Chili Bowl recently celebrated its 50th anniversary with a book, a celebration hosted by Bill Cosby, a block party, and a free concert at the 9:30 Club. Ben's is a surviving brand on a street of newer coffee shops, restaurants, bakeries, and bars. With its iconic menu supplemented with some healthier fare, Ben's Chili Bowl succeeds in serving the tastes of original patrons while cultivating the new.

Accommodating contemporary palates has become increasingly difficult for the family-run, neighborhood-based restaurants that serve favorites from African American heritage cooking. Cost, health, cosmopolitan appetites, and the presence of quick service restaurants mean that soulfood restaurants struggle for survival in some of the most historic black neighborhoods, even New York City's Harlem.

Although there are few recognized casual dining chain restaurants in historically black neighborhoods, in places that have had increased restaurant activity, neighbors associate it with imminent gentrification and the ultimate loss of the area. The success of those new restaurants may be a signal that invites new economic investment as well as municipal and corporate attention to areas in desperate need of it. That development inevitably changes the neighborhood and adds another chapter to the history.

Ben's Chili Bowl, Washington, D.C. AP Photo/Dennis Cook.

Soul food, fried chicken, greens, and macaroni and cheese, from Brownstone on Main, Columbus, Ohio. AP Photo/Jay LaPrete.

RESTAURANTS AND NEIGHBORHOODS

Manhattan residents were skeptical when Starbucks chairman Howard Schultz and NBA legend Magic Johnson announced plans to bring Starbucks to Harlem. Starbucks and Johnson's development corporation approved a limited agreement to open seven Starbucks shops near Johnson's theaters in black neighborhoods. In the spring of 1999, Starbucks opened in Harlem at 125th street and Malcolm X Boulevard. The partners paid special attention to particular details for customer comfort. They reinforced cultural history with design choices, the music, and the decision to stock sweet potato pie or peach cobbler. The shop was a symbol of the neighborhood's new economic era, and it appeared just as proprietors of restaurants from the previous era retired and residents wondered about the future of food in the neighborhood.[2]

Willette Craine Murray moved to New York from Charlotte, North Carolina, in 1933. She worked at Harlem's Theresa Hotel before opening the family-run restaurant and jazz club La Famille on Harlem's east side in 1958. The family sold the restaurant in 1989 and Willette Murray died six years later. Calvin Copeland opened one of Harlem's first catering businesses in 1958 on Broadway at West 148th Street. A restaurant worker by age 13, Copeland moved to New York from Virginia in 1945. Eventually the catering business expanded and Copeland's began serving the meals that made his restaurant legendary; it survived several riots, the waning popularity of jazz, a fire, and the drug wars, and it had become a regular stop on the neighborhood brunch tours. This generation of restaurateurs established their businesses as the legislative victories of the modern Civil Rights era raised expectations for another generation. The beneficiaries ascended to a tier of academic and professional choices that had been available to an elite segment of the black population.

That imagined social mobility inspired an identity politics to reinforce the coherence of the African American community. Soulfood quite literally belonged to a body of critical symbols of social identity that affirmed a place in community. Far from the physical boundaries of the community that members of this generation might travel, however, there would be cultural symbols to remind them of their origins. With high expectations for great change, many prospective professional cooks opened fast-food barbecue and soulfood shops in black neighborhoods. Young people who studied, worked, or lived outside black neighborhoods could walk down certain streets with notable restaurants to remember. The idea of soulfood proved an irreplaceable symbol uniting black Americans at a time when people feared that the

Chef Robert Williams serves the final Sunday brunch at Copeland's in Harlem. AP Photo/Louis Lanzano.

sense of community, as well as the tangible community, would disappear. New opportunities did change old neighborhoods and restaurant kitchens.

Harlem's resurgent economy—a former U.S. president's local office, increased value of housing stock, interest from chain stores and hotels—has raised the neighborhood's profile, as well as its rents and controversy surrounding it. Formulas that equate the arrival of The Body Shop in 1992 with the demise of Copeland's restaurant 15 years later are easy to make. The economics of the neighborhood have changed and the impact on business costs go beyond rent for the small family restaurant businesses that served the area. Compared with other parts of Manhattan, Harlem has historically had fewer restaurants. The absence of conventional restaurants created a space for home cooks to open lunch counters and storefronts, and for others to bring their food to the streets. They set up shop outside museums, churches, banks, and the phone company where they sold bean pies, yellow cake with chocolate frosting, meat pies and coco bread, and stews with starchy *foufou*.

Diners who would have chosen a restaurant had the choice been an option instead bought lunch from the vendors, further depressing the restaurant market but keeping foodservice in the area. Other barriers prevented a restaurant boom in Harlem. Nonprofit institutions are the strength of the neighborhood, and they anchored the area during the drug and health crises. By state law restaurants that serve liquor cannot be too close to churches and

De Angelo Evans at his cart outside New Haven's Union Station. Courtesy of the author.

schools, and Harlem has many churches. When opening a restaurant, one discovers that it is cheaper and easier to rent space that comes with intact commercial kitchen and ventilation system. Harlem's increasing rents suddenly made downtown venues more competitive, but more restaurateurs see a future in Harlem. They are encouraged by the area's demographic profile, the chain store interest, and the satisfaction of a having a place in an actual neighborhood. Ironically, their arrival coincides with the decline of the old style, family-run, soulfood restaurant in the area. Taste is as much a factor as economics in the disappearance of these restaurants, but it is a reality for black America's capital. It may eventually be the reality in other black neighborhoods across the country as restaurateurs find it more expensive to rent space and buy food while their regular patrons find it easier and cheaper to eat McDonald's, Chinese takeout, or supermarket prepared foods. For special occasions it is festive and healthier to dine at a casual chain restaurant or a white-tablecloth restaurant serving elegantly prepared, traditional favorites. Harlem's black residents have always had easy access to Manhattan's diverse range of culinary options, and they are beginning to have a similar range of choices in the neighborhood. That may nourish residents and Harlem, but it is too late for the old-style soulfood restaurant.

QUICK SERVICE AND FAST CASUAL RESTAURANTS

Many of the most familiar quick service restaurants have long histories with black consumers. McDonald's, Burger King, Wendy's, KFC, and others support black franchisees, have multiple locations in urban areas, and court consumers with comprehensive marketing campaigns. In 1968. Chicago-based Herman Petty became the first black owner/operator of a McDonald's franchise. With the guidance of Roland Jones, McDonald's first black regional department manager, black managers opened other McDonald's restaurants. As owner/operators discovered that their local networks helped to find effective solutions to common problems, they organized the National Black McDonald's Operators Association in 1972. McDonald's and other quick service restaurant leaders have been faithful to black communities and they are rewarded with clear brand loyalty.

Black Americans are identified as heavy users of quick service restaurants and score high in the categories that predict which Americans will be heavy users. Younger people and people with children favor quick service restaurants, and black Americans are well represented in each category. Restaurant researchers found African Americans 19 percent more likely than the general population to be quick service restaurant diners, but a smaller subset of the population, younger people and people without children, was likely to be both

Enjoying dessert out. Courtesy of the author.

heavy quick service restaurant diners and frequent sit-down diners. African Americans are well represented in the fast food or quick service customer base, but they also frequent both quick service restaurant chains and more formal restaurants, possibly fast casual, casual, white tablecloth, or upscale.[3]

Chinese food is becoming American diners' favorite ethnic cuisine, and that trend is reflected among black consumers. Black Americans heavily support the growth in Chinese food restaurants. Only seafood scored higher on a survey of monthly restaurant choices, but there is a correlation between the conveniently high numbers of Chinese takeout shops in urban areas and the high rates of black patronage. Food carts and street side vendors are reliable and trusted routes that culinary entrepreneurs followed to build recognition and gain capital for storefront or restaurant success in urban neighborhoods. Available, inexpensive real estate and minimal competition makes underserved black neighborhoods attractive markets for the determined culinary entrepreneur who is willing to invest in potentially transitional areas. Family-run Chinese takeout is a proven commodity in black communities. Proprietors agree to run businesses where others have not, and they have created a market niche while cultivating a palate with a balance of the familiar chicken, rice, beef, and pork with exotic tastes bounded by salty, sweet, or hot.

In busier commercial areas, the heavy foot traffic is incentive for street vendors and for the proprietors of storefront restaurants to claim the sidewalk with billboard signs, carts, and tables for the occasional al fresco diner and friends or patrons who meet, chat, and inevitably bring customers into the shop.

The vibrant street culture invariably attracts several versions of the mobile ice cream vendor, Good Humor or another, assured of an eager reception. African American consumer loyalty to quick service food, in various forms, is unquestioned. Black franchisees hold a small percentage of all quick service franchises, although the customer base is well established and major franchise restaurants offer programs to encourage black franchisees. Capital and saturation are obvious impediments to franchising, although they have not stopped the small family-run restaurants. Family-run shops, particularly those that serve Chinese food, have profited in black neighborhoods, simultaneously dispelling some myths about black consumers and the potential for business success even in economically marginal neighborhoods.

Prince Georges County, Maryland, a predominantly black region with a median household income of $55,256 (2000 Census), is an area that should have the perfect demographic for testing theories on restaurant dining patterns for black consumers. In this Washington, D.C., commuter suburb, residents can choose from the amenities of a cosmopolitan city, and they earn enough disposable income for regular meals at restaurants in any category. But if they are interested in fine dining or a selection of casual dining chains, Prince George's County residents go to another county or into the District. Casual and fancier chain restaurants are underrepresented in Prince George's County despite the fervent efforts of county officials and residents. The County's high concentration of black professionals shop, dine, and surrender their dollars in surrounding areas' upscale retail and seafood, Chinese, or steak chains. For residents and city officials it is an image problem, a service and amenities inconvenience, and a slight with revenue implications. The realities of Prince George's County's racial demographics mean that disappointed residents must wonder if racial bias is a factor in the county's inability to attract certain restaurants. Prince George's County is the most discussed example of restaurant under representation in black communities.

Magic Johnson's 1998 partnership with Carlson Restaurants Worldwide brought T.G.I. Friday's to an underserved Atlanta neighborhood. Together the companies planned to open T.G.I. Friday's locations in other underserved black neighborhoods of major American cities. Magic Johnson's initiative is aimed at stimulating investment in economically marginal black neighborhoods with restaurants and entertainment offerings that stabilize areas, foster a nurturing environment, and invite similar investment. Prince George's County is not economically marginal and residents complain that they are victims of a form of restaurant racial profiling that has been called "dining while black." Ad sales executives at urban radio stations fear that the pool of potential advertisers is unfairly restricted because of policies against urban dictates or marketing directly to black consumers in the black media. Some critics see the absence of casual dining chains as the result of an urban dictates policy. With minimal advertising, few locations, and a resistance to bringing casual and upscale dining chains to the most affluent black neighborhoods, intrepid black diners eventually assume the worst.[4]

Several dramatic controversies of the last decade played against the backdrop of a casual family style dining chain. Resulting misperceptions about African Americans as restaurant customers continue to influence the decisions made by restaurant location scouts to consider certain areas. Unhappy customers filed three separate class action lawsuits against Denny's Restaurants in the early 1990s. At trial, employees described such egregious examples of discriminatory behavior that the company's managers decided to settle with plaintiffs for $54 million, revamped policies, and federal monitoring. Denny's has since become a leader in fostering workplace diversity and the company successfully reengaged disenchanted black consumers with good faith efforts to groom black managers, work with diverse suppliers, and treat all customers with dignity. Denny's is not the only major restaurant chain to face this kind of public relations battle. The Equal Employment Opportunity Commission (EEOC) on behalf of customers and employees filed a workplace discrimination suit against the Cracker Barrel Old Country Store restaurant chain for racial discrimination in 2004.

The EEOC investigation documented humiliating episodes for black employees who were also assigned to serve black customers when white employees refused. The restaurant settled the suit two years later with a financial fund and antidiscrimination policies in the workplace. The settlement and operational policy change was the second in a year for the company, which settled a class action suit brought by the civil rights organization, the National Association for the Advancement of Colored People, and wronged African American customers. The positive resolution to these lawsuits serves the interests of the victims but has little effect on the restaurant situation in black neighborhoods or the cultural conflicts that magnify concerns about doing business there.[5]

Market researchers know that African American diners favor Chinese food and seafood more than the population generally and are more frequent customers at steak houses. This knowledge has not translated into new restaurants, and scholars of hotel and restaurant management and diversity issues wonder about the logic of these decisions. Cultural factors in addition to the financial questions are influencing the decision to locate casual chain restaurants in black neighborhoods. Perceptions of neighborhood safety and economic stability would affect staffing and the ability to attract customers who live outside the neighborhood. The belief that local diners could not afford the restaurant or the total restaurant experience with appetizers, entrées, dessert, possibly drinks, and tip is an issue as well. For black diners the legacy of the entire history of service can be recalled because of a bad dining experience. That history means that some customers are highly sensitive. In many ways integrated dining is a recent phenomenon and many black diners remember that history. In a busy restaurant, it is easy for customers to feel slighted and wait staff to become frustrated. From an imperfect seat, to a long wait, to a disagreement over the proper temperature for hot food, different expectations about service make the restaurant dining room the setting for unexpectedly complex race relations. Long waits between visits from the server could be the result of a busy server with too many tables, and it could be that the server is busy and chooses to give the table of African Americans less attention. And it could be a little of both.

For black diners the meal can be equally fraught with negative situations. Culinarily conservative and expecting a certain standard of service—at the level a family member might offer another—some diners approach unfamiliar restaurants warily. The menu choices may be unappetizing, the restaurant dining room—where they are in the minority—can feel uncomfortable, the server may not be patient enough especially with a menu that requires interpretation, and there is the question of what good restaurant service is worth. These factors combined make location an initial issue in the complex of race and restaurants. It is an incredible opportunity to push along a subtle civil rights issue in America, but it has also served a network of nicer restaurants that serve familiar favorites in an elegant setting. They are safe choices for dinners out and special occasions, and the proprietors may be happy not to compete with well-funded chain restaurants. The absence of casual dining chains in black neighborhoods means fewer diners there are introduced to new restaurants and the food trends they popularize. Barriers to the next level of dining, the upscale restaurant, are magnified to the point of reinforcing the original misperceptions and myths.[6]

NOTES

1. Dick Cluster, *They Should Have Served that Cup of Coffee: Seven Radicals Remember the '60s* (Cambridge, MA: South End Press, 1979); Harvard Sitkoff, *The Struggle for Black Equality, 1954–1992*, rev. ed. (New York: HarperCollins, 1993).

2. Larry Platt, "Magic Johnson Builds an Empire: The Former Laker Great Is Dragging White Businesses into Inner Cities, Fulfilling What He Calls His 'Black Plan,'" *The New York Times Magazine*, December 10, 2000.

3. Julie O'Donnell, *Dining Out Is Quintessentially American: The Scarborough Restaurant Report* (New York: Scarborough Research, 2006); A. Elizabeth Sloan, *What, Where, and When America Eats: State of the Industry Report* (Chicago: Institute of

Food Technologists, 2006); Timothy Williams, "In Changing Harlem, Pig's Feet and Greens Lose Spots on Menu," *The New York Times*, August 6, 2008.

4. Michael Barbaro and Krissah Williams, "Prince George's Makes Sales Pitch for High-End Retail," *The Washington Post*, June 1, 2005; Thomas M. Shapiro, *The Hidden Cost of Being African American: How Wealth Perpetuates Inequality* (New York: Oxford University Press, 2004); Dona J. Stewart, "Hot 'lanta's Urban Expansion and Cultural Landscape Change," *The Geographical Review* 89 (1999): 132–140; David H. Kaplan, "The Uneven Distribution of Employment Opportunities: Neighborhood and Race in Cleveland, Ohio," *Journal of Urban Affairs* 21, no. 2 (1999): 189–212; Gregory D. Squires and Charis E. Kubrin, *Privileged Places: Race, Residence, and the Structure of Opportunity* (Boulder, CO: Lynne Rienner Publishers, 2006).

5. Faye Rice and Anne Faircloth, "Denny's Changes Its Spots," *Fortune Magazine*, May 13, 1996.

6. Michael Lynn, "Ethnic Differences in Tipping: A Matter of Familiarity with Tipping Norms," *Cornell Hospitality Quarterly* 45, no. 1 (2004): 12–22; Kim Severson, "Dining While Black: Why in a City as Diverse as San Francisco Are most Patrons in Upscale Restaurants White?" *The San Francisco Chronicle*, December 30, 2001.

BIBLIOGRAPHY

Barbaro, Michael, and Krissah Williams. "Prince George's Makes Sales Pitch For High-End Retail." *The Washington Post*, June 1, 2005.

Cluster, Dick. *They Should Have Served that Cup of Coffee: Seven Radicals Remember the '60s*. Cambridge, MA: South End Press, 1979.

O'Donnell, Julie. *Dining Out is Quintessentially American: The Scarborough Restaurant Report*. New York: Scarborough Research, 2006.

Platt, Larry. "Magic Johnson Builds an Empire: The Former Laker Great is Dragging White Businesses into Inner Cities, Fulfilling what He Calls His 'Black Plan.'" *The New York Times Magazine*, December 10, 2000.

Severson, Kim. "Dining While Black: Why in a City as Diverse as San Francisco are most Patrons in Upscale Restaurants White?" *The San Francisco Chronicle*, December 30, 2001.

Shapiro, Thomas M. *The Hidden Cost of Being African American: How Wealth Perpetuates Inequality*. New York: Oxford University Press, 2004.

Sitkoff, Harvard. *The Struggle for Black Equality, 1954–1992*, rev. ed. New York: Harper-Collins, 1993.

Sloan, A. Elizabeth. *What, Where, and When America Eats: State of the Industry Report*. Chicago: Institute of Food Technologists, 2006.

Squires, Gregory D. and Charis E. Kubrin. *Privileged Places: Race, Residence, and the Structure of Opportunity*. Boulder, CO: Lynne Rienner Publishers, 2006.

6

Special Occasions

Holiday celebrations amplify black America's relationship to national identity. Preservation of religious and cultural traditions made it possible for black people to survive and eventually thrive in America. Those same customs are connections to ancestors and histories that most black American families will never fully know. A growing number are able to celebrate births, christenings, engagements, special birthdays, and other milestones with such culturally specific details as family stories, rediscovered traditions, or special foods because of scientific genealogical research and the assistance of local history projects. Church-based, cultural, historical, and Neo-African celebrations affirm the significance of the African American journey as the nation and its people change.

Author and antislavery activist Frederick Douglass questioned the relevance of the Fourth of July for enslaved blacks in the years before emancipation, but time and political progress have made that date, Memorial Day, Labor Day, and the other patriotic holidays fully accepted celebrations for black families. This distinction—American realities with the inflections of African American history—shapes celebrations of church anniversaries, historic neighborhood festivals, and the reinvigorated observances of Juneteenth, originally a recognition of the day that enslaved blacks in Texas discovered that slavery had ended. For many celebrations, heritage cuisine or signifying food—foods that are recognizably tied to familiar aspects of history, culture, and folklore—is the essential ingredient that affirms the authenticity of an annual event. As people, politics, demographics, and daily situations change, cultural celebrations and the signifying foods reinforce the stability of tradition. Foods prepared and served at these events add coherence to events that have deep roots in African American history and have been a source of sustenance from slavery to the present. Through these adaptive celebrations and the foods that are served, African Americans affirm an indigenous culture and identity.[1]

The earliest cookbooks and domestic guides produced by blacks recorded professional wisdom from a gentleman's butler or a cook in a wealthy nineteenth-century home. The genre that followed documents holidays, special occasions, and celebrations and it remains a solid category for black cookbooks. Sue Bailey Thurman and her colleagues at the National Council of Negro Women recognized the relationship between cooking and preserving history and produced a book to share historical facts and connections to food at the same time that activists were demanding historic change in the country. They published *The Historical Cookbook of the American Negro* in 1958, several years after the Montgomery bus boycotts and the Kansas school desegregation decision but just before the North Carolina lunch counter sit-ins or the March on Washington. It is a record of African American history realized in recipes that emerged just as the world was changing radically. It captured a legacy and held it safe during a period when critics called many of these traditions, figures, and foods anachronistic. This book and others like it restore traditions just as family holiday recipes preserve memories and family choices reflect the persistence of a legacy against the centrifugal pull of American society. African Americans' signifying foods and the efforts to preserve them through holiday celebrations and similar events enhance the common culture of the United States.

MAJOR HOLIDAYS

Familiarly observed holidays among African Americans are the major religious and secular holidays for many Americans. In secular or religious ways, many Americans recognize the two major religious holidays, Christmas and Easter, and the nation's religious holidays of Thanksgiving and the Fourth of July. In each of these celebrations the primary differences are in the style of worship and the meal. Defining factors of the Christmas meal are heavily influenced by region and local tradition. Remnants of the nineteenth-century *Réveillon* celebration survive in contemporary New Orleans at nightly restaurant buffets held at the city's premier restaurants during Christmas week. Creole families inherited the French Catholic tradition and finished midnight mass on Christmas Eve with an elaborate feast of gumbo, shellfish, soufflés, beef terrines, beef grillade, grits, eggs, puddings, wine, and liqueurs. Families had an equally grand meal on New Year's Eve.[2]

Alternatively, Nation of Islam (NOI) leader Elijah Muhammad chose December for the Nation's Ramadan observance because Christmas was so dominant. Praying regularly, observing a dry fast until sunset, and abstaining from poultry and meat are all expected during Ramadan. The fast ends with juice, water, or fruit and an evening meal that is vegetarian, although past restrictions on potatoes, kale, and other vegetables complicate vegetarian cooking. In 1998, NOI leader Louis Farrakhan moved the observance of Ramadan from December to the month—usually in early fall—defined by the Islamic calendar and orthodox Muslim custom. NOI followers now observe Ramadan with Muslims worldwide, although some continue to practice the December fast.

Christmas is a commercial holiday, but for devout African Americans it is a religious celebration of the savior's birth to be shared with family and friends. Contemporary commercial Christmas is a twentieth-century innovation, and there is an African American generation that remembers simpler holidays with extended family where a reasonably extravagant meal was the focus of the family celebration. Cooking the special meal with extra attention to family favorites was a central part of the holiday festivities that might begin with supper on Christmas Eve, include a special breakfast with visiting family, and continue with dinner and some events through the week. Contemporary African American families balance the commercial and religious aspects of Christmas with home cooks, taking the opportunity to cook dishes from inherited recipes, incorporate new foods or the wishes of new family member, recognize regional delicacies, and accommodate the holiday imperatives seen in magazines or on television. A family celebration with a well-decorated tree and plenty of gifts is not complete without the major meal and extended family on Christmas Day. A successful meal means that guests felt they could contribute a dish prepared with their own family's recipes. The ideal meal is supplemented with side dishes, desserts, and parts of the main course brought to the meal by friends and family members.

Guests greet each other and catch up on news with an appetizer course of deviled eggs, cheeses, crackers, chips, nuts, vegetables, and dips. At the seated dinner table there is plenty of meat with roasted, smoked, or deep-fried turkey and stuffing, ham, and possibly beef. Macaroni and cheese, sweet potatoes, a tomato dish, green beans, collard or turnip greens, mashed potatoes, a corn, dish, and possibly black-eyed peas are all acceptable as side dishes along with some regional specialty or the family favorite that every good cook can prepare. Yeast dinner rolls, cornbread, or biscuits are part of the meal along with a range of carbonated beverages, sodas, fruit drinks, tea, beer, and liquor. Children have their own junior table and are expected to eat a good portion of the evening's meal, although gifts from Santa Claus and other distractions make that nearly impossible.

The dessert course is another chance for the ambitious home cook to prove his or her mettle, so pound cakes, banana puddings, sweet potato pies, and lemon meringue pies brought by friends surround the host's contribution to the dessert table. The celebration continues through the week between Christmas and New Year's with Kwanzaa, the feast of first fruits. Visiting friends and family may mean that the ambitious host takes time during the week to prepare chitterlings or another labor-intensive legacy dish.

Reinvigorated festivals are historic celebrations updated to suit the needs of the twenty-first century community. Kwanzaa is a conscious amalgam of West African religious practices and the political imperatives of the twentieth-century black activists who imagined it. Kwanzaa is a Swahili term that means first fruits. Ron Karenga, a political and cultural activist, introduced the holiday in 1966 as an alternative to Christmas. The celebration occurs nightly for the seven nights between Christmas and New Year's, making it easy to keep both Christmas and Kwanzaa. Food is prominently featured in Kwanzaa with the table setting that evokes African and American heritage through African textiles, a ceremonial candleholder and cup, and candles in the black unity colors, red, black, and green. The table is dressed with nuts, fruits, and vegetables of the first harvest.

Kwanzaa's seven principles are *umoja* (unity), *kujichagulia* (self-determination), *ujima* (collective work and responsibility), *ujamaa* (cooperative economics),

Tonel LaKay Dance and Drum ensemble from Haiti perform at the New York Museum of National History. AP Photo/Jennifer Szymaszek.

nia (purpose), *kuumba* (creativity), and *imani* (faith). Families light a candle and discuss the day's principle. A performance might lead from the solemn exercise into the celebratory meal and gift exchange. Because the holiday is so defined by symbolism, the food served can be as precise in its representation of African and American cultural contributions. Offerings come from the West African and the African American culinary traditions. A possible menu might include West African Jollof rice or another composed rice dish, Caribbean chicken curry or chicken yassa from Senegal, green beans, turnips, nuts, fruit, with sweet potato pie and lemon pound cake for dessert. Because the holiday unfolds over seven nights, there is room for the ambitious cook to experiment. Community groups sponsor Kwanzaa celebrations with a potluck or covered dish meal and during a busy holiday season a family might observe Kwanzaa at home the first night and attend a community center celebration for other nights. For the truly vigilant, Kwanzaa requires a substantial commitment to cooking, and there are good cookbooks to guide the novice through the seven nights of food and ritual. Kwanzaa is an invented tradition drawn from harvest imagery. For seven nights it is carried along on the culinary traditions of African Americans. It is the most recent and possibly the most precise example of the ways African American culinary traditions influenced and sustained holiday practices.

Black-eyed peas. Courtesy of the author.

Pound Cake

1/2 cup butter, room
  temperature
1 1/4 cups white sugar
1 1/2 teaspoons lemon zest
1/2 teaspoon orange zest
3 large eggs, room
  temperature
1 teaspoon vanilla

2 cups all-purpose flour
1/2 teaspoon baking soda
1 teaspoon baking powder
1/2 teaspoon of salt
1/4 cup sour cream, room
  temperature
1/2 cup cream cheese, room
  temperature

Preheat oven to 350° F.

(1) Mix the dry ingredients except sugar together in a small bowl and set aside. Grease and flour an 8 × 4 loaf pan. In a large bowl blend the butter, and cream cheese until fluffy, then add sugar and blend thoroughly. (2) Add eggs to the dairy mixture and continue blending. After the eggs pour in the vanilla and the lemon zest. (3) Next add the remaining dry ingredients to the larger bowl and pour in the sour cream. Continue blending until the ingredients are well mixed and the batter is pale yellow. (4) Pour batter into greased and floured loaf pan and bake in 350° F oven for 35 minutes to an hour depending on the oven. Cake is finished when the center is firm and a toothpick or knife inserted into the middle emerges clean. (5) Cake should cool and can be pried from the loaf pan or left in the pan to be sliced and removed as it is eaten.

New Year's Eve is the week's culminating activity, with many families spending some part of the night at church for the Watch Night Service. The night's worship service of prayer, meditation, and song welcomes midnight and the arrival of a New Year. John Wesley, a founding leader in the Methodist church, encouraged his eighteenth-century congregations to share in regular watch night or covenant services. The witness of Moravian Christians led him to adopt the practice that black church leaders, Methodist and Baptist, easily adapted. By the late nineteenth century Watch Night services were a New Year's Eve tradition for Southern and Midwestern Methodist white churches, as well as black congregations.

Attending a Watch Night Service makes it easy to enjoy a festive midnight snack or late supper of Hopping John, the black-eyed peas and rice dish, for good luck in the coming year and collard greens for prosperity. Secular friends who greet the New Year in other ways catch up on the black-eyed peas, rice, greens, cornbread, a succotash of beans and corn, and okra later that afternoon at successive open houses hosted by friends and family to welcome the New Year and share a final visit with departing relatives.

Easter, the other major religious holiday, is a smaller and more solemn observance again focused on worship with the secular interruptions of dyed Easter eggs, baskets, new spring outfits, and Easter Bunny candy. For black Catholics living along the Louisiana coast, gumbo z'herbes is a customary Lenten meal served on Holy Thursday or Good Friday. The green gumbo, theoretically vegetarian for the fast, is made with five, seven, nine, or eleven different kinds of greens. An odd number of greens is lucky and the number of greens in the pot is the number of new friends to be made that year.

Gumbo Z'herbes

A New Orleans Tradition on Holy Thursday

1 bunch mustard greens	1/2 cup garlic, chopped
1 bunch collard greens	1 1/2 gallons water
1 bunch turnip greens	6 tablespoons flour
1 bunch watercress	1 pound smoked turkey or
1 bunch escarole	turkey parts
1 bunch arugula	1 pound hot chicken sausage
1 bunch broccoli rabe	1 teaspoon ground sage
1 bunch spinach	1 teaspoon thyme
1 bunch beet greens	prepared rice
3 cups onions, diced	Salt and black pepper to taste

(1) Rinse greens thoroughly, making sure to pick out bad leaves, and to rinse away any soil. Then wash them again, and probably once more. Chop up the greens and place all except the arugula, and escarole in a large pot with onions, garlic, and water. Once the pot is boiling, reduce the heat to simmer, and cook covered for 15 to 20 minutes. In a small pan, brown the flour by sautéing it over a low heat. Once it is approaching the color of light brown sugar, it is ready. Remove from the stove and set aside. (2) Remove greens and reserve their cooking liquid. Puree the greens in a food processor or blender and mix in the 6 tablespoons of flour. Chop the meats into small pieces and cook in the greens liquid over a low heat. When the meat has thoroughly cooked for 20 minutes, bring the greens back to the pot with the spices. (3) The gumbo should cook covered over a very low heat for another 40 minutes. Liquid levels may need adjusting; if so add a little more water. Stir regularly to prevent sticking and burning on the bottom of the pan. (4) Salt and pepper to taste and serve with rice.

Easter lunch or dinner is a smaller gathering than Christmas or Thanksgiving. It can be a grander version of the regular Sunday dinner and is rarely on the scale of the large family meals during the major holidays. Lamb is now a popular main course, but a more traditional menu with ham, chicken, or a roast is more representative. Again regional specialties distinguish the meal as well as seasonal vegetables. Easter Sunday is the incentive for some church volunteer groups to host special breakfasts for early services or lunch after a mid morning service. A special Easter brunch buffet at a popular restaurant is an alternative to the weekly Sunday dinner.[3]

The Fourth of July and Thanksgiving are the nation's holidays that all citizens can share regardless of most religious obligations. The Fourth of July is a summer holiday and the best reason to picnic and grill outdoors. The observance of this holiday would be hard to prevent. The Fourth is the perfect holiday showcase for the workhorses of African American heritage cookery: barbecue ribs, fried chicken, and potato salad. Easily transported, durable, and delicious, fried chicken moved through history from platters on plantations, to public markets and train station vending stalls, to box lunches for travel in segregated America. Its long and iconic journey through American history should ensure its place at Fourth of July celebrations. Along with those expected dishes, there will be burgers and hot dogs—turkey, beef, chicken, or vegetarian options—for grilling, and chips and sodas—orange, grape, and red, or berry. Fresh corn, Cole slaw, macaroni salad, green salad, pasta salad, pickles, peppers, and relish, as well as an exotic salad of international origin, would all join the potato salad. In areas where fresh fish or seafood is a seasonal treat, fish is part of the meal, too. Ice cream, cobbler made with fresh peaches, chocolate cake, strawberry shortcake, and fresh fruit, certainly watermelon, complete the Fourth of July cookout.

Thanksgiving, like Christmas, brings families together from various parts of the country but without the religious symbolism or the commercial charge that accompanies Christmas. The absence of religious orthodoxy makes the holiday a perfect time to focus on family stories and customs. Those advantages are good incentive to make an exhausting journey to a family Thanksgiving dinner. The meal is similar to a Christmas dinner with a mix of favorites, heritage dishes, and standard Thanksgiving fare. A main course of turkey, chicken, and ham is usual. Sweet potatoes, turnips and their greens, and other seasonal vegetables remind everyone that this is an autumn meal. Cornbread, sausage, or plain sandwich bread stuffing are favorites that are enriched with thick gravy and served with mashed potatoes, tomatoes, and green vegetables. Regional specialties such as corn pudding, smoked oyster stuffing, squash pie, and special requests to accommodate vegetarians or religious restrictions all personalize the meal even more. Desserts are a mix of familiar sweets as well as apple pie and other fall favorites, but the classic sweet potato pie usually trumps pumpkin.

Bubba Charles and crew prepare a cookout at Yale University. Courtesy of the Yale University Office of New Haven and State Affairs.

FAMILY AND COMMUNITY CELEBRATIONS

Observances of Labor Day, Memorial Day, and other national holidays emphasize the choices black Americans have made in support of the nation. Community and family celebrations are declarations of the sacrifices and joys that made it possible to imagine a black community. Weddings, family reunions, and funerals bring families together, subsume differences, and create opportunities to recapture history and reflect on its value until another milestone offers the chance to repeat the exercise. The strength of the wedding market made planning guides focused on African American heritage inevitable. The popularity of Harriette Cole's 1993 guide, *Jumping the Broom: The African American Wedding Planner*, repositioned an antebellum marriage symbol for contemporary brides. This guide, another one, or a wedding planner helps the bride choose a location, the official, the décor, invitations, entertainment, attire, and the reception.

Many couples now include a broom ceremony in the wedding service and search for the intrepid caterer who will accept the charge of planning a menu that appeals to a multiethnic, black crowd by serving foods from the African Diaspora that must satisfy guests with African American, West Indian, and West African culinary roots. The wedding feast unites two families and needs to incorporate various traditions. A bride may want favorite candies as a wedding favor and the groom may request the Caribbean black cake, a rich spicy fruit pastry, for his groom's cake. Their wedding meal specifications can be rich with symbolism: appetizer course of black-eyed pea fritters, crab cakes, and Jamaican vegetable patties with a main course of rice, a corn, okra, and tomato dish, sautéed mixed greens, the Brazilian chicken stew *ximxim de galinha*, roasted sweet potatoes with chilies, followed by fresh fruit and the signature wedding cake from *Jumping the Broom*. That cake, with its four hexagonal tiers iced in gold and white frosting in a *kente* cloth inspired pattern, generated enough inquiries that wedding cake bakers have a substitute or a good replica of the broom cake ready as a response. Such an ambitious menu unites cultures, references journeys, and anticipates the varied temperatures and flavors of a marriage to reflect the personalized traditions so evident in contemporary weddings.

Families are trading up from the old afternoon picnic family reunion to destination weekends and longer vacations on cruise ships or international resorts. As the events blossom, the core mission of reconnecting with family and documenting history is easy to miss. The most basic reunion is centered on activities to bring distant relatives together, free time for reminiscing, a fun family outing, worship service to remember the dead, and plenty of good food. A cookout or picnic for one of the meals ensures a variety of choices for vegetarians or for family members who do not eat pork or watch their cholesterol, salt, or sugar. A fish fry combines two traditions, although the fish fry only needs a group that appreciates fish. A fish fry is a little more work than a picnic and people expect whiting, porgy, or catfish to be served. A fried whiting dinner is completed with tartar sauce, hot sauce, French fries, Cole slaw, macaroni and cheese, cornbread, or cornmeal hush puppies. It is hard work that may even be better ordered from a caterer or restaurant, but for many a fish fry symbolizes celebration and community.[4]

Weddings and reunions celebrate beginnings and connections, but food can be equally rich with symbolism when it is part of a mourning ritual for the end of a human life. African-derived cultures across the Diaspora have highly choreographed pageants for mourning loved ones. Soon after slavery ended, free blacks formalized mutual aid and burial societies to care for each other in sickness and death. Some societies disappeared, others grew into prosperous social organizations, and others are still secret societies that appear unexpectedly at funerals to sing, shout, pray, and occasionally parade the descendant of an original member home. It is hard to comfort in the midst of a funeral, but food is essential and the assurance that food is available helps when a family is planning and mourning. Pies and cakes materialize automatically, but the family and their visitors must also eat meals. A ham, roast chicken, potatoes, spinach, or green beans are all acceptable food to send or bring during mourning. The culinary standard or comparable meal is Sunday dinner. The intensive prep reserved for a holiday meal would be extravagant, but a Sunday dinner dish is appropriate. Meals or components that store or freeze well are also sent. A funeral or memorial is a reunion and an opportunity for signifying foods to comfort, remind, and sustain.

Choices that shape weddings, funerals, reunions, and other family gatherings remind participants that culture and tradition, especially within families, are not static. They continually incorporate, update, and adapt. Favorite foods represent a stable element that through preparation can change slightly while lending historical integrity to a new or revised tradition. Blacks have centuries of history in America that activists and historians reexamine for clues to daily life. As community groups and cultural activists understood more about enslaved blacks' holidays and celebrations, the events seemed to commemorate activities worthy of recognition today. Emancipation Day, black election festivities, and Juneteenth moved from obscurity into a place in the cultural programming of many black communities. These observances are regional, but they are gaining wider recognition and forcing history enthusiasts to track down other forgotten holidays.

Abraham Lincoln freed enslaved blacks in Washington, D.C. on April 16, 1862, the year before the Emancipation Proclamation. Free blacks in the District recognized that date as a holiday with parades, speakers, and activities from the end of the Civil War through the beginning of the twentieth century. Blacks in Virginia learned that they were free much later and they celebrated Emancipation Day in September. News of freedom reached Texas even later, making Juneteenth celebrations possible. Reinvigorating these regional observances united nineteenth-century political sensibilities and twentieth-century public program patterns. Organizers' response to the parades, speeches, and family activities of the nineteenth century is quite often to present updated versions hosted by a cultural institution with an exhibition, performance, lecture, and hands-on family activities. Creative menu planning legitimated these events through the authenticity of foodways. Recipes exist for the election day cake that blacks in eighteenth-century New England shared at their spring celebration and for Emancipation Proclamation Day cake, but organizers of these contemporary celebrations wisely chose to include traditional favorites or innovative dishes made with familiar ingredients that guests recognize immediately. The astute presentation of history through public programs reinforced with foods that symbolize African

American heritage passed historic, nineteenth-century festivals to another generation.

(Easy) Red Rice

2 1/2 cups prepared rice (it
  is possible to find frozen
  prepared rice)
1 can 14.5 oz diced tomatoes
1 small onion chopped
1 teaspoon garlic

1/4 cup tomato salsa,
  medium or hot
1 can 6.5 oz minced clams
1 tablespoon fresh parsley
  chopped roughly
3 tablespoons olive oil

(1) In medium saucepan warm the oil over a low heat and once it is hot add the onion and garlic. Cook until they are clear and soft and add the tomatoes, salsa, parsley and cook for 5 minutes. (2) Pour in prepared rice and clams, cover and cook until rice is colored and infused with the sauce. Check on the rice regularly. It will burn if left without stirring.

NOTES

1. James A. Colaiaco, *Frederick Douglass and the Fourth of July* (New York: Palgrave Macmillan, 2006); William H. Wiggins, *O Freedom! Afro-American Emancipation Celebrations* (Knoxville: University of Tennessee Press, 1987).

2. Bettye Collier-Thomas, *A Treasury of African-American Christmas Stories* (New York: Henry Holt & Company, October 1997); William H. Wiggins and Douglas DeNatale, *Jubilation! African American Celebrations in the Southeast* (Columbia: University of South Carolina Press, 1994).

3. Elizabeth H. Pleck, *Celebrating the Family: Ethnicity, Consumer Culture, and Family Rituals* (Cambridge, MA: Harvard University Press, 2000); Antoinette Broussard, *African American Celebrations and Holiday Traditions* (New York: Citadel, 2004); Ramon A. Gutierrez, *Feasts and Celebrations in North American Ethnic Communities* (Albuquerque: University of New Mexico Press, 1995).

4. Gary Lee, "The Family Reunion Trip: It's All Relatives From Big-City Hotels to Tropical Islands, African Americans Are Thinking Big," *The Washington Post*, January 8, 2006; Krystal Williams, *How To Plan Your African-American Family Reunion* (New York: Citadel, 2000); Donna Beasley, *The Family Reunion Planner* (New York: John Wiley & Sons 1997).

BIBLIOGRAPHY

Beasley, Donna. *The Family Reunion Planner*. New York: John Wiley & Sons, 1997.

Broussard, Antoinette. *African American Celebrations and Holiday Traditions*. New York: Citadel, 2004.

Colaiaco, James A. *Frederick Douglass and the Fourth of July*. New York: Palgrave Macmillan, 2006.

Collier-Thomas, Bettye. *A Treasury of African-American Christmas Stories*. New York: Henry Holt & Company, October 1997.

Gutierrez, Ramon A. *Feasts and Celebrations in North American Ethnic Communities* Albuquerque: University of New Mexico Press, 1995.

Pleck, Elizabeth H. *Celebrating the Family: Ethnicity, Consumer Culture, and Family Rituals*. Cambridge, MA: Harvard University Press, 2000.

Thurman, Sue Bailey, ed., and the National Council of Negro Women. *The Historical Cookbook of the American Negro*. 1958. Reprint, Boston: Beacon Press, 2000.

Wiggins, William H. *O Freedom! Afro-American Emancipation Celebrations*. Knoxville: University of Tennessee Press, 1987.

Williams, Krystal. *How to Plan Your African-American Family Reunion*. New York: Citadel, 2000.

7

Diet and Health

George Tillman Jr.'s 1997 movie *Soul Food* brought an intracommunity conversation about food and health in black America to a wider audience. The movie's most sympathetic character, a long-suffering black matriarch who keeps her family together with a weekly Sunday dinner, dies because she does not manage her diabetes. To some viewers and critics the filmmaker seemed to be saying soul food was killing African America. The alarming rates of high blood pressure, certain types of cancer, high cholesterol, and diabetes were not secrets. The number of people affected meant most blacks knew someone or had a family member at risk of or living with a chronic disease. Musicians B. B. King, Patti LaBelle, and Marvin Isley live with diabetes. Gladys Knight, The Blind Boys of Alabama, and Indianapolis Colts coach Tony Dungy are involved with the American Diabetes Association's campaigns for black Americans.

Talk radio, magazines, and health care organizations emphasized the importance of an improved diet as a strategy for preventing chronic illness in children and adults. Public health researchers at universities, foundations, and insurers committed resources to education and prevention of obesity and the weight-related risks of diabetes, stroke, and heart attack. In partnership with churches, community organizations, and genealogical groups, nonprofit health organizations analyzed behavior, shared strategies for change, and promoted the findings. Black America is a young population. The 2006 census estimate for median age is 31 years, and that is a motivating factor in public health circles. Success in disease prevention now will avoid more costly disease treatment later.

HEALTH RISKS IN AFRICAN AMERICA

The relative ease of contemporary American life—grocery store prepared foods, affordable automobiles, fewer physically demanding jobs in manufacturing or farming—have made it easier to eat more while doing less physically. Too much food and too little physical activity are a national concern, but it is an extreme situation for blacks. Health data from 2003 to 2004 revealed that 67 percent of adults in the age group 20–70 years are overweight and 34 percent are obese. An estimated 60 percent of African American men and 78 percent of women in the age group 20–70 years can be described as overweight. The figures for obesity are also higher than desired, and this condition, intensified by minimal health insurance and related healthcare disparities, leads to hypertension, diabetes, and chronic illness. The urban grocery gap and the high number of quick service restaurants in urban areas are contributing factors along with too little exercise and excess fats, salt, and sugar found in some prepared foods and in home cooking. Convenience, cost, and targeted marketing make African Americans a highly valued customer base for McDonald's, Burger King, and other fast food brands. The combined advertising amount directed to African Americans and Latinos is estimated to be more than $3 billion. This is an ideal market because of the high number of younger families with children. Some studies suggest that fast food advertising is more likely to appear during shows that are popular with African American audiences, in magazines with an African American adult reader base, and even in grocery stores in black neighborhoods.[1]

Almost 30 percent of American adults have high blood pressure, and although there is normally some increase in blood pressure levels with age, the condition disproportionately affects black Americans. Hypertension, chronic high blood pressure, is a factor for 35 percent of African Americans who are twice as likely to die as a result of the condition than Americans of European descent. Hypertension appears earlier in life for African American patients, which means living with and managing the condition longer, possibly half a lifetime. Risks of heart disease—the leading cause of death for black Americans—kidney disease, and stroke also increase as a result of high blood pressure. Genetics, stress, physiology, and certainly diet all play a role in controlling blood pressure. Too much weight, a high salt diet, lack of exercise, extreme psychological stress, and regularly drinking alcohol put one at high risk.

African Americans seem predisposed to the condition even when many of these factors are not relevant. There is great speculation and some researchers consider it a genetic puzzle. Surprisingly, a comparative study of Nigerians, African Americans, and black Jamaicans showed lower rates of hypertension in the Nigerian and Jamaican sample population. Although genetics accounted for conditions that made high blood pressure more likely, black people who ate a limited diet with few processed foods and little salt, engaged in physical labor, maintained leaner bodies, and presumably had a different type of stress did not develop hypertension. There is more to discover about the environmental, physiological, and genetic factors that aggravate a hypertensive condition in African Americans.[2]

The prognosis for diabetes is equally dire. It is the sixth leading cause of death in America, and an estimated 20 million people over the age of 20 have diabetes. Close to 3 million African Americans over the age of 20 have diabetes, although it may be underdiagnosed. Diabetes, "the sugar" in black American vernacular, results in high levels of blood glucose when the body has difficulty with insulin production. It can lead to serious health complications that include blindness, heart disease, kidney failure, extremity amputation, and premature death.

Blacks suffer from several forms of cancer that may be influenced by diet. Colorectal cancer follows lung, breast, and prostate cancer as another deadly health threat. Health officials estimated that of the 152,000 new cases of cancer diagnosed in 2007, colorectal cancer would be found in 9 percent of the men and 12 percent of the women. Mortality rates for African American men and women with colorectal cancer remained steady for a decade while the rates for men and women of European descent decreased. Diagnosis at an earlier stage and fewer barriers in accessing proper treatment would improve survival rates. Also, nutrition issues that result from what is sometimes called the "African-American diet" favor the conditions that lead to hypertension and diabetes. It is now commonly accepted that most if not all African Americans are lactose intolerant or minimally have problems with digestion. This misperception can be a factor in the insufficient calcium and dairy levels that add to the risk of chronic disease.

With a diet that is higher in fats and meats, many black Americans are missing essential vitamins and minerals, including calcium, found in fruits, vegetables, grains, and dairy products. Dietary guidelines recommend that regular consumption of low-fat dairy products, vegetables, and fruits will help prevent chronic illness. Although three-fourths of African Americans may have some problem with lactose digestion that results in gastrointestinal difficulties, there are effective strategies that make digestion possible.[3] Data compiled by the African American Lactose Intolerance Understanding Study show that the condition does not require eliminating necessary dairy from an otherwise healthy diet. Study subjects were able to drink 8 ounces of milk twice a day with the proper preparation. Milk, along with many other foods, is a factor in the accumulated health concerns facing black America and can be part of the solution to those problems.

HEALTH AND AFRICAN AMERICAN HERITAGE COOKING

With all the bad news on nutrition and diet-related health hazards, it is easy to blame the food. Traditional foods and the favored methods of preparation can, in combination with other factors, contribute to poor health. The actual food is not the problem; in fact many are quite nutritious. Preferences in cooking style produce many of the hazards in the foods that arrive on the plate. These foods are full of nutrients in their raw form. Certain cherished practices magnify the levels of sodium and fat to unhealthy levels while eliminating the nutritional benefits of the raw ingredients. With time, guidance, and practice, cooking techniques can be adapted and healthier practices substituted in without too much difference in flavors. Many cooks understand the proposed changes but need practice to redirect their cooking reflexes away from the practices that add fat, increase cholesterol, and rob the food of its nutritional value.

Butter, margarine, trans-fat oils, and lard infuse fried chicken with a deep, rich flavor, make flaky piecrusts and biscuits, and condense into syrup for candied sweet potatoes. Unsaturated margarine and shortenings introduce a different flavor but produce a biscuit filled with the same delicate layers that regular shortening makes. Deep-fat frying, with its antecedents in West Africa and Europe, has been linked to pancreatic and colorectal cancers. Oven frying or baking skinless poultry coated with herbs and breadcrumbs is a healthier alternative. Choosing oils and shortening that is low in saturated fats instead of regular vegetable oil or shortening does not change the taste radically and adds a minimal amount of harmful fats when sautéing. Vegetable and chicken broths, fruit or vegetable juice, and cooking spray in place of oils enhance flavor and lubricate the pan without the risk of carcinogens from high heat and oil cooking. Substituting egg whites for the whole egg reduces fat and limiting sugar and replacing salt with other seasonings, herbs, or flavors are all cooking improvements that make traditional dishes healthier. Eating smaller portions and fewer servings of red meat makes an occasional indulgence acceptable. Implementing these kinds of changes gives the favorites of African American heritage cuisine a chance to be healthy again.

HEALTHY FOODS

Foods that survived over generations belonged to a culinary culture based on farm fresh produce, seasonal eating, and locally raised meat, poultry, and fish. Dietitians, public health researchers, local agriculture activists, and food writers praise this kind of eating as the solution to most of the society's food-related health problems. Fresh produce, prepared conservatively, is an essential component of any effort to prevent food-related chronic illness. Sweet potatoes, both the pale cream-colored variety and the deep orange twin, are native to the Americas and belong to the Ipomoea family. They are not yams, although that is often how they are labeled in grocery stores. A true yam is a pale, hairy-skin tuber that is native to Africa and belongs to the Dioscorea family. A cognate to the English word yam exists in Spanish, Portuguese, and in several West African languages, attesting to the plant's journey. Fresh sweet potatoes are typically part of a fall harvest, but they are also available canned. They are rich in vitamins A and C, an antioxidant that fights the damage that can lead to heart disease and diabetes.

Collard, mustard, and other leafy greens are standards of black vernacular cooking that are naturally healthy. Hours of simmering over a low heat with high fat meat minimize the calcium, iron, and vitamins A and C found in the greens. Sautéing thinly sliced greens in a broth with extra flavoring or cooking traditionally for shorter time with poultry or flavorful seasonings conserves more nutrients. They are at their peak in fall and winter, but fresh collards are in grocery stores year round. Calcium deficiency is a concern for hypertensive individuals, and leafy greens, cooked properly, help minimize this risk. Black-eyed peas, the species *Vigna unguiculata*, are high in protein and can be a good source of iron and fiber. They are rich in potassium, a therapeutic mineral for hypertensive individuals. Lightly cooked and well seasoned, black-eyed peas are a delicious addition to salads and stews.

Black-eyed Pea and Quinoa Salad

1 16 oz bag frozen black-eyed peas	1 cup chopped fennel (optional)
1 16 oz bag frozen okra	2 cups water or broth for quinoa
1 cup quinoa (Peruvian grain)	1 tablespoon olive oil
1 medium sweet onion, ideally Vidalia (optional)	Juice of one lime
3 ears fresh corn	1/2 teaspoon ground cumin
1 small tomato chopped	1/4 teaspoon cayenne pepper
1 small cucumber chopped	1/4 cup vinegar
	1 tablespoon chopped parsley or cilantro

(1) In a large pan bring water to boil and successively cook the corn, black-eyed peas, and okra in the pan, removing each food and reserving the water before adding the next. Each ingredient should cook for no more than 10 minutes once the water is boiling. Once corn is cool, cut the kernels from the cob into a large bowl. (2) In another pot bring 2 cups of water or broth to boil, add quinoa and reduce heat. Cover pot and let quinoa simmer until the water is absorbed. The quinoa burns quickly so stirring and

(continued)

checking is advised. (3) Mix olive oil, limejuice, vinegar, and spices in a small bowl or covered jar. Add quinoa, peas, fennel, onion (if using) okra, cucumber, and tomato to the large bowl of corn. Pour in olive oil dressing, toss salad, and adjust dressing to suit taste. Refrigerate the covered salad until ready to serve.

Black-eyed peas, collards, and sweet potatoes are a nutritious and easy addition to all kinds of meals. Because it is a little slick and acrid tasting, okra may not be a favorite vegetable, but it carries valuable nutrients that help lower cholesterol and balance the risk of heart disease. The fiber decreases the colorectal cancer risk and okra has impressive levels of potassium and calcium. Sautéed, quick fried, or blanched okra enhances a salad or a corn, tomato, onion medley.

Fruits and fruit flavors are cherished in African American cooking. Lemon, orange, grape, and cherry are comfortingly familiar flavors found in foods that begin the day at the breakfast table and proceed right through to dessert. The appeal of fruit flavorings, however, is often reduced to an orange soda that yields little nutritional value. Fresh fruit is convenient, nutrient loaded, and delicious. Watermelon is full of antioxidant vitamins C and A, and it does not need cooking, so heart disease- and colon cancer-fighting nutrients are not compromised. Bananas, peaches, apricots, oranges, and other fruits often baked into cobblers, pies, and other desserts are naturally loaded with potassium. Served fresh, prepared as shortcake, or in another recipe emphasizing the goodness of fresh produce, these fruits retain their nutrients and escape being overwhelmed by sugary syrups. Soulfood is beleaguered, although some critics are beginning to distinguish between the food, the actual ingredients, and the modes of cooking. Besieged though soulfood might be, its demise is unimaginable. Efforts to adapt the style of cooking and to make it healthier are inevitable. As a result of the campaign to reposition the ingredients, black-eyed peas, collard greens, sweet potatoes, and other healthy favorites may move out of the ethnic culinary category and into the healthy one.[4]

PROGRAMS FOR PREVENTION

Physician and celebrity journalist Ian Smith spent Saturday April 7, 2007 with singers Patti LaBelle, Yolanda Adams, and hundreds of supporters on the Mall in Washington, D.C. They were in the District to launch a public health program sponsored by State Farm Insurance to inspire black America to lose 50 million pounds. The 50 Million Pound Challenge is a major

African American public health initiative with the ambitious goal of improved health for millions of people over a three-year period. State Farm and Smith brought the campaign to the people with stops in Oakland, Cleveland, New York, and 11 other cities in its first year. Taking the Challenge is easy to do online at the Challenge Web site where there are tools for tracking and posting weight loss, and checking on progress with friends and neighbors. Kits are also available from local State Farm agents. To reach individuals at risk and demonstrate prevention strategies, public health intervention programs target both the national and neighborhood level.

State Farm's sponsorship of this promotion is a sign of the high cost of preventable chronic illness. Targeted appeals covering African Americans' health issues are not a new endeavor for insurers or healthcare organizations. Aetna Insurance produces a popular black health issues calendar profiling news and advances among healthcare professionals and in healthcare delivery. An early calendar recognized African American heritage cooking and the health issues logically followed. The 50 Million Pound Challenge differs in the investment and the methodology. By using pop culture patterns understood through reality TV and for-profit weight loss centers, the Challenge activates a broader base. Through a campaign that rivals a McDonald's product rollout, a quarter of a million participants signed up, entered data online, and reported a collective weight loss of 1 million pounds in the first seven months. The enthusiasm generated by this initiative brought a renewed interest to companion programs devoted to the same work on a smaller scale.

Across America community groups, churches, schools, social groups, healthcare providers, and celebrities are partnering in the fight against diabetes, hypertension, and other food-related illness. With the divisive reality of racial disparities in healthcare—African Americans receive a different standard of healthcare—these types of public health initiatives are socially good while being savvy marketing. High-profile efforts with national aspirations, major corporate sponsorship, and celebrity cheerleaders fit into a growing industry organized around African American health issues. The challenge of improving the situation unites grassroots program leaders, government officials, corporate managers, and healthcare providers.

Creative community-based partnerships between local university hospitals, medical schools, and neighboring nonprofits bring the public health lessons to patients in the immediate neighborhoods. Many promising studies begin effectively, but finding ways to help subjects maintain behavior patterns after a grant cycle ends is difficult. Researchers at Baylor College partnered with African American Boy Scout Troops in Houston in 1997 to develop the 5 a Day Achievement Badge to teach the essential role of fruits and vegetables for good health. The medical researchers provided comprehensive support for the scouts who had fast low-fat, simple, safe, and tasty recipes available, trainings and tastings to explain the food groups, themed-comic books to reinforce the demonstrations, and a mini-program to gauge parental involvement in the study. The scouts who completed the program received the badge. This study and similar scout programs in other states succeeded in exposing adolescent boys to the importance of fruits, juice, and vegetables in their diets. The scouts with badges understood the value of the foods and knew how to prepare healthy snacks with them. Engaging the parents in the program proved more difficult and their eating, shopping, and cooking habits will define any continuous 5-a-day regimen.[5]

A Johns Hopkins University School of Public Health study brought health-care resources to 300 hypertensive African American men of diverse ages in Baltimore. A population typically underserved and assumed to be hard to reach, the men were actually very interested in better health and eager to participate. The lead investigator worried that ultimately it might take the resources of a village to reduce blood pressure levels on a large scale. Because many of the men used hospital emergency rooms as their primary care facility, the cost of community-based resources for prevention education, health assessment, and patient follow-up monitoring could still be cheaper than the emergency room visits of patients with chronic hypertension or diabetes.[6]

Public health managers at the federal level are creating national programs informed by university studies and grassroots community projects. *Power to Prevent: A Family Lifestyle Approach to Diabetes Prevention* is a project of the Centers for Disease Control and Prevention, the National Institutes of Health, and the National Diabetes Education Program that assigns responsibilities for improving health to community groups, churches, and similar neighborhood institutions. The philosophy is based on a model that uses public campaigns, partnership networks, community interventions, and health systems to reach special populations. The program goals stress widespread comprehension of diabetes prevention facts: weight management, physical activity, and healthy eating. The *Power to Prevent* curriculum brings the goal of improved physical fitness into a formal class environment.

Church-based programs stress peer education and monitoring especially in men's and women's organizations. Programs run by and for female church leaders who are not ministers are authoritative models for larger national initiatives because they have quantifiable results.

Churches and other voluntary affiliations perform a critical role as conduits in prevention efforts. Parishioners choose to belong to a church and remain in the community because they are valued and respected. A church member's status within the worship community may be much higher than in other parts of his or her life, and that affirmation keeps the member doing more for the church. As a church leader, participation in a weight loss program or another healthier lifestyle project has greater meaning because of the community leader status. At work or in another venue these same leadership qualities may be unrecognized.

Churches and social organizations are logical places to base educational efforts, as food, particularly traditional food, plays a pivotal role in many church activities and celebrations. As more churches and the congregational leaders discuss healthier cooking and lifestyles along with serving healthier foods at church events, members of the congregation will understand the urgency and adapt their cooking at home.

Roasted Sweet Potatoes with Chilies

5–7 medium sweet potatoes,
  preferably the orange
  Beauregard or Hernandez,
  but the Jersey White is fine
1/4 cup chili peppers
1/2 cup olive oil

1 1/2 tablespoons fresh
  cilantro, chopped
3 tablespoons garlic, minced
2 teaspoons ground rosemary
Pinch of kosher salt
Baking sheet

Preheat oven to 400° F.

(1) Peel the potatoes and cut into bite-sized chunks. Roughly chop the peppers into smaller pieces being careful not to touch face or eyes before washing hands. (2) Arrange the potatoes on the baking sheet allowing a little space between them. Sprinkle the potatoes with chopped chilies. Apply olive oil to potatoes and chilies and season them with garlic and rosemary. (3) Roast in 400° F oven for 20 to 40 minutes. Check the potatoes regularly so the smaller pieces do not burn. When potatoes are fully cooked, remove them and chilies from the oven and toss in a bowl with olive oil, salt, and cilantro.

NOTES

1. National Center for Health Statistics, *Health, United States, 2007 With Chartbook on Trends in the Health of Americans* (Hyattsville, MD: National Center for Health Statistics, 2007); Sonya A. Grier, Janell Mensinger, Shirley H. Huang, Shiriki K. Kumanyika, and Nicolas Stettler, "Fast-Food Marketing and Children's Fast-Food Consumption: Exploring Parents' Influences in an Ethnically Diverse Sample," *American Marketing Association* 26, no. 2 (2007): 221–235.

2. Richard S. Cooper, Charles N. Rotimi, and Ryk Ward, "The Puzzle of Hypertension in African-Americans," *Scientific American*, February 1999, 56–63; Osagie K. Obasogie, "Hypertension: What Oprah Doesn't Know," *The Los Angeles Times*, May 17, 2007; Jay Kaufman, "The Anatomy of a Medical Myth," *Social Science Research Council*, June 7, 2006, http://www.raceandgenomics.ssrc.org/; Philip D. Curtin, "The Slavery Hypothesis for Hypertension among African Americans: The Historical Evidence," *American Journal of Public Health* 82, no. 12 (1992): 1681–1686.

3. Wilma J. Wooten and Winston Price, "The Role of Dairy and Dairy Nutrients in the Diet of African Americans," *Journal of National Medical Association* 96, no. 12 (2004): 20S–24S; L. J. Appel, T. J. Moore, E. Obarzanek, W. M. Vollmer, L. P. Svetkey, F. M. Sacks, G. A. Bray, T. M. Vogt, J. A. Cutler, M. M. Windhauser, P. H. Lin, and N. Karanja, "A Clinical Trial of the Effects of Dietary Patterns on Blood Pressure," *The New England Journal of Medicine*, 336, no. 6 (1997): 1117–1124.

4. Claudia Kalb and Anna Kuchment, "Saving Soul Food; Health-conscious African-Americans Are Reinventing Classic Recipes. So Long, Pork Fat; Hello, Baked Chicken," *Newsweek*, January 30, 2006.

5. Tom Baranowski, Baranowski Janice; Karen W. Cullen, Carl deMoor, LaTroy Rittenberry, David Hebert, and Lovell Jones, "5 a Day Achievement Badge for African-American Boy Scouts: Pilot Outcome Results 1," *Preventive Medicine* 34 (2002): 353–363; Shannon N. Zenk, Amy J. Schulz, Teretha Hollis-Neely, Richard T. Campbell, Nellie Holmes, Gloria Watkins, Robin Nwankwo, and Angela Odoms-Young, "Fruit and Vegetable Intake in African Americans: Income and Store Characteristics," *American Journal of Preventive Medicine* 29, no. 1 (2005): 1–9.

6. Ming Tai, "Urban African-American Men and Blood Pressure," *The JHU Gazette* 33, no. 12 (2003); Martha Hill, "Hypertension Care and Control in Underserved Urban African American Men: Behavioral and Physiologic Outcomes at 36 Months," *American Journal of Hypertension* 16, no. 11 (2003): 906–913; C. R. Dennison et al., "Underserved Urban African American Men: Hypertension Trial Outcomes and Mortality during Five Years," *American Journal of Hypertension* 20, no. 2 (2007): 164–171.

BIBLIOGRAPHY

Appel, L. J., T. J. Moore, E. Obarzanek, W. M. Vollmer, L. P. Svetkey, F. M. Sacks, G. A. Bray, T. M. Vogt, J. A. Cutler, M. M. Windhauser, P. H. Lin, and N. Karanja. "A Clinical Trial of the Effects of Dietary Patterns on Blood Pressure." *The New England Journal of Medicine* 336 (1997): 1117–1124.

Baranowski, Tom, Janice Baranowski, Karen W. Cullen, Carl deMoor, LaTroy Rittenberry, David Hebert, and Lovell Jones. "5 a Day Achievement Badge for African-American Boy Scouts: Pilot Outcome Results 1." *Preventive Medicine* 34, no. 3 (2002): 353–363.

Cooper, Richard S., Charles N. Rotimi, and Ryk Ward. "The Puzzle of Hypertension in African-Americans." *Scientific American*, February 1999, 56–63.

Curtin, Philip D. "The Slavery Hypothesis for Hypertension among African Americans: The Historical Evidence." *American Journal of Public Health* 82, no. 12 (1992): 1681–1686.

Hill, Martha. "Hypertension Care and Control in Underserved Urban African American Men: Behavioral and Physiologic Outcomes at 36 Months." *American Journal of Hypertension* 16, no. 11 (2003): 906–913.

Kalb, Claudia and Anna Kuchment. "Saving Soul Food; Health-Conscious African-Americans Are Reinventing Classic Recipes. So Long, Pork Fat; Hello, Baked Chicken." *Newsweek*, January 30, 2006.

Wooten, Wilma J., and Winston Price. "The Role of Dairy and Dairy Nutrients in the Diet of African Americans." *Journal of National Medical Association* 96, no. 12 (2004): 20S–24S.

Resource Guide

GENERAL WORKS

Baer, Hans and Yvonne Jones, eds. *African Americans in the South: Issues of Race, Class, and Gender.* Athens: University of Georgia Press, 1992.

Bates, Karen Grigsby and Karen Elyse Hudson. *Basic Black: Home Training for Modern Times.* New York: Doubleday, 1996.

Bower, Anne L., ed. *African American Foodways: Explorations of History and Culture.* Urbana: University of Illinois Press, 2007.

Carney, Judith. *Black Rice: The African Origins of Rice Cultivation in the Americas.* Cambridge: Harvard University Press, 2001.

Curtin, Deane W. and Lisa Heldke. *Cooking, Eating, Thinking: Transformative Philosophies of Food.* Bloomington: Indiana University Press, 1992.

Davidson, Alan. *The Penguin Companion to Food.* New York: Penguin Press, 2002.

Dornenberg, Andrew and Karen Page. *Becoming a Chef: With Recipes and Reflections from America's Leading Chefs.* New York: Van Nostrand Reinhold, 1995.

Grauer, Anne L. *Bodies of Evidence: Reconstructing History Through Skeletal Analysis.* New York: Wiley-Liss, 1995.

Haber, Barbara. *From Hardtack to Home Fries: An Uncommon History of American Cooks and Meals.* New York: The Free Press, 2002.

Kamp, David. *The United States of Arugula: How We Became a Gourmet Nation.* New York: Broadway Books, 2006.

Keller, Linda and Kay Mussell. *Ethnic and Regional Foodways in the United States: The Performance of Group Identity.* Knoxville: University of Tennessee, 1984.

Kelley, Robin D. G. *Freedom Dreams: The Black Radical Imagination.* Boston: Beacon Press, 2002.

Kurlansky, Mark. *Big Oyster: History on the Half Shell.* New York: Ballantine, 2006.

Lanchester, John. *The Debt to Pleasure*. New York: Henry Holt and Company, 1996.

Levenstein, Harvey. *Revolution at the Table: The Transformation of the American Diet*. New York: Oxford University Press, 1988.

Masumoto, David M. *Epitaph for a Peach: Four Seasons on my Family Farm*. New York: HarperOne, 1996.

Masumoto, David M. *Four Seasons in Five Senses: Things Worth Savoring*. New York: W. W. Norton and Company, 2004.

Menzel, Peter and Faith D'Aluisio. *Hungry Planet: What the World Eats*. Napa, CA: Material World Press and Ten Speed Books, 2005.

Mintz, Sidney W. *Tasting Food, Tasting Freedom: Excursions into Eating, Culture, and the Past*. Boston: Beacon Press, 1996.

Nestle, Marion. *What to Eat*. New York: North Point Press, 2006.

Patel, Raj. *Stuffed and Starved: The Hidden Battle for the World Food System*. Brooklyn: Melville House Publishing, 2008.

Ruhlman, Michael. *The Elements of Cooking: Translating the Chef's Craft for Every Kitchen*. New York: Scribner, 2007.

Shange, Ntozake. *If I Can Cook, You Know God Can*. Boston: Beacon Press, 1998.

Thornton, John. *Africa and Africans in the Making of the Atlantic World, 1400–1800*, 2nd ed. Cambridge, UK: Cambridge University Press, 1998.

Tisdale, Sallie. *The Best Thing I Ever Tasted: The Secret of Food*. New York: Riverhead Books, 2000.

Toussaint-Samat, Maguelonne. *A History of Food*. translated by Anthea Bell. Cambridge, MA: Blackwell Publishers, 1992.

Turner, Patricia A. *Ceramic Uncles and Celluloid Mammies: Black Images and their Influence on Culture*. New York: Anchor Books, 1994.

COOKBOOKS

Angelou, Maya. *Hallelujah! The Welcome Table: A Lifetime of Memories with Recipes*. New York: Random House, 2004.

Armstrong, Govind. *Small Bites, Big Nights: Seductive Little Plates for Intimate Occasions and Lavish Parties*. New York: Clarkson Potter, 2007.

Bowers, Lessie. *Plantation Recipes*. New York: Robert Speller & Sons, 1959.

Bowser, Pearl and Joan Eckstein. *A Pinch of Soul*. New York: Avon, 1970.

Broussard, Antoinette. *African American Celebrations and Holiday Traditions*. New York: Citadel, 2004.

Brown, Warren. *Cakelove: How to Bake Cakes from Scratch*. New York: Stewart Tabori & Chang, 2008.

Butler, Cleora. *Cleora's Kitchens and Eight Decades of Great American Food*. Tulsa: Council Oak, 1986.

Butts, Calvin O. *Food for the Soul: Recipes and Stories from the Congregation of Harlem's Abyssinian Baptist Church*. New York: One World/Ballantine, 2005.

Chase, Leah. *And Still I Cook*. Gretna, LA: Pelican Publishing, 2003.

Chase, Leah. *The Dooky Chase Cookbook*. Gretna, LA: Pelican Publishing, 1990.

Copage, Eric V. *Kwanzaa*. New York: William Morrow, 1991.

Council, Mildred. *Mama Dip's Family Cookbook*. Chapel Hill: University of North Carolina Press, 2007.

Darden, Norma Jean and Carole Darden. *Spoonbread and Strawberry Wine*. New York: Ballantine Books, 1978.

De Knight, Freda. *A Date with a Dish: A Cookbook of American Negro Recipes*. New York: Hermitage Press, Inc., 1948.

Edwards, Gary. *Onj E Fun Ori Sa (Food for the Gods)*. New York: Yoruba Theological Archministry, 1981.

Fearnley-Whittingstall, Hugh. *The River Cottage Meat Book*. New York: Ten Speed Press, 2007.

Garvin, Gerry. *Turn up the Heat with G. Garvin*. Des Moines: Meredith Books, 2006.

Hall, H. Franklyn. *300 Ways to Cook and Serve Shellfish: Terrapin, Green Turtle, Snapper, Oysters, Oyster Crabs, Lobsters, Clams, Crabs and Shrimps*. Philadelphia: Christian Banner, 1901.

Harris, Jessica B. *The Africa Cookbook: Tastes of a Continent*. New York: Simon & Schuster, 1998.

Harris, Jessica B. *Beyond Gumbo: Creole Fusion from the Atlantic Rim*. New York: Simon & Schuster, 2003.

Harris, Jessica B. *Iron Pots and Wooden Spoons: 175 Authentic Cajun, Creole, and Caribbean Dishes*. New York: Ballantine Books, 1989.

Harris, Jessica B. *A Kwanzaa Keepsake: Celebrating the Holiday with New Traditions and Feasts*. New York: Simon & Schuster, 1998.

Harris, Jessica B. *The Martha's Vineyard Table*. San Francisco: Chronicle Books, 2007.

Harris, Jessica B. *The Welcome Table: African-American Heritage Cooking*. New York: Simon & Schuster, 1995.

Henderson, Jeff. *Cooked: From the Streets to the Stove, From Cocaine to Foie Gras*. New York: William Morrow Co., 2007.

Hendricks, Bobby. *Barbeque with Mr. Bobby Que*. Memphis: Wimmer Brothers, 1976.

Holland, Tanya. *New Soul Cooking: Updating a Cuisine Rich in Flavor and Tradition*. New York: Stewart, Tabori & Chang, 2003.

Hultman, Tami and Africa News Service. *The Africa News Cookbook: African Cooking for Western Kitchens*, Revised Edition. New York: Penguin, 1986.

Jeffries, Bob. *Soul Food Cook Book*. Indianapolis: Bobbs-Merrill Company, 1969.

Jones, Wilbert. *The New Soul Food Cookbook: Healthier Recipes for Traditional Favorites*. New York: Citadel, 2005.

Kaiser, Inez Yeargan. *Soul Food Cookery*. New York: Pitman Publishing, 1968.

Knight, Gladys. *At Home with Gladys Knight: Her Personal Recipe for Living Well, Eating Right, and Loving Life*. Alexandria, VA: American Diabetes Association, 2001.

Kuffman, Dorothy, ed. *West Oakland Soul Food Cookbook*. Oakland, CA: Peter Maurin Neighborhood House, 1969.

LaBelle, Patti. *Patti LaBelle's Lite Cuisine: Over 100 Dishes with To-Die-For Taste Made With To-Live-For Recipes*. New York: Gotham Books/Penguin Group, 2004.

Lewis, Edna. *The Edna Lewis Cookbook*. New York: The Ecco Press, 1972.

Lewis, Edna. *In Pursuit of Flavor*. New York: Alfred A. Knopf, 1988.

Lewis, Edna. *The Taste of Country Cooking*. New York: Alfred A. Knopf, 1976.

Lewis, Edna and Scott Peacock. *The Gift of Southern Cooking: Recipes and Revelations from Two Great American Cooks*. New York: Alfred A. Knopf, 2003.

Lyford, Carrie Alberta. *A Book of Recipes for the Cooking School*. Hampton, VA: Press of the Hampton Normal and Agricultural Institute, 1921.

Medearis, Angela Shelf. *The African-American Kitchen: Cooking from Our Heritage*. New York: Dutton, 1994.

Mendes, Helen. *The African Heritage Cookbook*. New York: Macmillan Publishing Company, 1971.

Paige, Howard. *Aspects of Afro-American Cookery*. Southfield, MI: Aspects Publishing Company, 1987.

Pinner, Patty. *Sweets: Soul Food Desserts and Memories*. Berkeley: Ten Speed Press, 2006.

Randall, Joe and Toni Tipton-Martin. *A Taste of Heritage: The New African American Cuisine*. New York: Wiley, 2002.

Ruhlman, Michael and Brian Polcyn. *Charcuterie: The Craft of Salting, Smoking, and Curing*. New York: W. W. Norton & Company, 2005.

Samuelsson, Marcus. *The Soul of a New Cuisine: A Discovery of the Foods and Flavors of Africa*. New York: Wiley, 2006.

Sanders, Dori. *Dori Sanders' Country Cooking: Recipes and Stories from the Family Farm Stand*. Chapel Hill, NC: Algonquin Books of Chapel Hill/Workman Publishing, 1995.

Smalls, Alexander and Hettie Jones. *Grace the Table: Stories and Recipes from my Southern Revival*. New York: HarperCollins, 1997.

Smart-Grosvenor, Vertamae. *Vibration Cooking of the Travel Notes of a Geechee Girl*. New York: Ballantine Book, 1970.

Smith, B. B. *Smith: Rituals and Celebrations*. New York: Random House, 1999.

Spivey, Diane M. *The Peppers, Cracklings, and Knots of Wool Cookbook: The Global Migration of African Cuisine*. Albany: State University of New York Press, 1999.

Tillery, Carolyn Quick. *Southern Homecoming Traditions: Recipes and Remembrances*. New York: Citadel, 2006.

Tuesday Magazine. *The Tuesday Magazine Soul Food Cookbook*. New York: Bantam, 1969.

Turner, Bertha, Katherine Tillman, and Kate Baker. *The Federation Cookbook: A Collection of Tested Recipes, Contributed by the Colored Women of the State of California*. Pasadena: 1910 reissued Carlisle, MA: Applewood Books, 2007.

Waddles, Charleszetta. *The Mother Waddles Soul Food Cookbook*. Detroit: Perpetual Soul Saving Mission for all Nations, 1970.

Williams, Lindsey. *Neo Soul: More than 100 Tempting Recipes*. New York: Avery/Penguin Group, 2007.

Winder, Delilah. *Delilah's Everyday Soul: Southern Cooking with Style*. Philadelphia: Running Press Book Publishers, 2006.

Woods, Marvin. *The New Low-Country Cooking: 125 Recipes for Coastal Southern Cooking with Innovative Style.* New York: William Morrow Cookbooks, 2000.

Woods, Sylvia. *Sylvia's Family Soul Food Cookbook: From Hemingway, South Carolina to Harlem.* New York: William Morrow Cookbooks, 1999.

Young, Bob, Al Stankus, and Deborah Feingold. *Jazz Cooks: Portraits and Recipes of the Greats.* New York: Stewart, Tabori & Chang, 1992.

WEB SITES

Aetna African American History Calendar, www.aetna.com/diversity/aahcalendar/2008/index.html.

Carolina Gold Rice Foundation, www.carolinagoldricefoundation.org.

Cuisine Noir online magazine, www.cuisinenoir.com.

David Walker Lupton African American Cookbook Collection, The University of Alabama, www.lib.ua.edu/lupton/luptonlist.htm.

Eat in Harlem, Your Guide to Eating in Harlem, www.eatinharlem.com.

Fearless African Americans Connected and Empowered Angie Stone and Eli Lilly and Company, www.face-diabetes.com/face/index.html.

Fifty Million Pound Challenge, www.50millionpounds.com/.

Multicultural Foodservice & Hospitality Alliance, www.mfha.net.

North American Farmer's Direct Marketing Association, www.nafdma.com/FMC2/.

Real Men Cook culinary showcase and fundraiser, www.realmencook.com.

Smithsonian Institution Traveling Exhibition Service Exhibit, "Key Ingredients: America by Food," www.keyingredients.org/.

United States Department of Agriculture Food and Nutrition, www.usda.gov and www.my pyramid.gov.

FILM

Daughters of the Dust. 1991. Dir. Julie Dash. Kino Video.

Frank's Place. David Chambers, Richard Dubin, and Tim Reid. 1987. CBS Corporation.

I'll Fly Away. Joshua Brand and John Falsey. 1991. National Broadcasting Company.

Imitation of Life. Douglas Sirk. 1959. Universal Home Entertainment.

Imitation of Life. John M. Stahl. 1934. Universal Home Entertainment.

Kickin' Chicken. Joy Phillips. 2001. Available at www.youtube.com.

Killer of Sheep. Charles Burnett. 1977. Milestone Film and Video.

Last Holiday. Wayne Wang. 2006. Paramount.

The Long Walk Home. Richard Pearce. 1990. Miramax Films.

Soul Food. George Tillman, Jr. 1997. 20th Century Fox

What's Cooking? Gurinder Chadha. 2000. Lion's Gate.

Selected Bibliography

Baranowski, Tom et al. "5 a Day Achievement Badge for African-American Boy Scouts: Pilot Outcome Results 1." *Preventive Medicine* 34 (2002): 353–363.

Belasco, Warren. *Appetite for Change: How the Counterculture Took on the Food Industry. 1966–1988.* New York: Pantheon, 1989.

Carney, Judith. *Black Rice: The African Origins of Rice Cultivation in the Americas.* Cambridge, MA: Harvard University Press, 2001.

Cooper, Richard S., Charles N. Rotimi, and Ryk Ward. "The Puzzle of Hypertension in African-Americans." *Scientific American*, February 1999, 56–63.

Darden, Norma Jean, and Carole Darden. *Spoonbread and Strawberry Wine.* New York: Ballantine Books, 1978.

Davidson, Alan. *The Penguin Companion to Food.* New York: Penguin Press, 1999.

De Knight, Freda. *A Date with a Dish: A Cookbook of American Negro Recipes.* New York: Hermitage Press, 1948.

Du Bois, W.E.B. *The Philadelphia Negro: A Social Study.* Philadelphia: University of Pennsylvania Press, 1899.

Franklin, Maria. "The Archaeological and Symbolic Dimensions of Soul Food: Race, Culture and Afro-Virginian Identity." In *Race and the Archaeology of Identity*, ed. Charles Orser. Salt Lake City: University of Utah Press, 2001.

Hall, Gwendolyn Midlo. *Africans in Colonial Louisiana: The Development of Afro-Creole Culture in the Eighteenth Century.* Baton Rouge: Louisiana State University Press, 1992.

Harris, Jessica. *The Welcome Table: African-American Heritage Cooking.* New York: Simon & Schuster, 1995.

Hess, Karen. *The Carolina Rice Kitchen: The African Connection.* Columbia: University of South Carolina Press, 1992.

Isaac, Rhys. *The Transformation of Virginia, 1740–1790*. New York: W. W. Norton & Company, 1982.

Littlefield, Daniel C. *Rice and Slaves: Ethnicity and the Slave Trade in Colonial South Carolina*. Urbana: The University of Illinois Press, 1991.

Levenstein, Harvey. *Revolution at the Table: The Transformation of the American Diet*. New York: Oxford University Press, 1988.

Levenstein, Harvey. *Paradox of Plenty: A Social History of Eating in Modern America*. New York: Oxford University Press, 1993.

Lewis, Edna. *The Taste of Country Cooking*. New York: Alfred A. Knopf, 1976.

O'Donnell, Julie. *Dining Out Is Quintessentially American: The Scarborough Restaurant Report*. New York: Scarborough Research, 2006.

Osseo-Asare, Fran. *Food Culture in Sub-Saharan Africa*. Westport, CT: Greenwood Press, 2005.

Pleck, Elizabeth H. *Celebrating the Family: Ethnicity, Consumer Culture, and Family Rituals*. Cambridge, MA: Harvard University Press, 2000.

Randall, Joe and Toni Tipton-Martin. *A Taste of Heritage: The New African American Cuisine*. New York: Wiley, 2002.

Sampson, A. E., S. Dixit, A. F. Meyers, and R. Houser Jr. "The Nutritional Impact of Breakfast Consumption on the Diets of Inner-City African-American Elementary School Children." *Journal of the National Medical Association* 87, no. 3 (1995): 195–202.

Sanders, Dori. *Dori Sanders' Country Cooking: Recipes and Stories from the Family Farm Stand*. Chapel Hill, NC: Algonquin Books of Chapel Hill/Workman Publishing, 1995.

Shapiro, Thomas M. *The Hidden Cost of Being African American: How Wealth Perpetuates Inequality*. New York: Oxford University Press, 2004.

Sitkoff, Harvard. *The Struggle for Black Equality, 1954–1992*, rev. ed. New York: HarperCollins, 1993.

Sloan, A. Elizabeth. *What, Where, and When America Eats: State of the Industry Report*. Chicago: Institute of Food Technologists, 2006.

Smart-Grosvenor, Vertamae. *Vibration Cooking of the Travel Notes of a Geechee Girl*. New York: Ballantine, 1970.

Williams-Forson, Psyche. *Building Houses out of Chicken Legs: Black Women, Food, and Power*. Chapel Hill: University of North Carolina Press, 2006.

Winne, Mark. *Closing the Food Gap: Resetting the Table in the Land of Plenty*. Boston: Beacon Press, 2008.

Witt, Doris. *Black Hunger: Soul Food and America*. Minneapolis: University of Minnesota Press, 1999.

Index

About the Author

WILLIAM FRANK MITCHELL is an instructor in the Urban and Community Studies Department at the University of Connecticut, West Hartford.

DATE DUE
